Daniel's Music

One Family's Journey from Tragedy to Empowerment through Faith, Medicine, and the Healing Power of Music

By Jerome Preisler with the Trush Family

Skyhorse Publishing

Skyhorse Publishing books may be purchased in bulk at special discounts for sales promotion, corporate gifts, fund-raising, or educational purposes. Special editions can also be created to specifications. For details, contact the Special Sales Department, Skyhorse Publishing, 307 West 36th Street, 11th Floor, New York, NY 10018 or info@skyhorse-publishing.com.

Skyhorse® and Skyhorse Publishing® are registered trademarks of Skyhorse Publishing, Inc. ®, a Delaware corporation.

www.skyhorsepublishing.com

10 9 8 7 6 5 4 3 2 1

Library of Congress Cataloging-in-Publication Data is available on file.

ISBN: 978-1-62087-694-7

Printed in the United States of America

Contents

ACKNOWLEDGMENTS

Many people have played a role in our family's journey since the unforgettable Sunday afternoon of March 9, 1997, and we are most appreciative of all of you. We are also thankful to the individuals who helped bring our story to life.

We would like to acknowledge all those who, beyond making a great difference in our lives, took the time to share their recollections with Jerome Preisler during the writing of this book through interviews, e-mails, and ongoing conversations. In alphabetical order:

Dr. Rick Abbott, whose professionalism, dedication, and perseverance helped Daniel turn the corner during that critical first month at Beth Israel Hospital.

Robert Bernstein, a special friend, for printing out and giving us the entire Daniel's Update Guestbook as a keepsake before it was taken off line and lost forever. The Guestbook was invaluable for piecing together our timeline and the wonderful updates used in our book.

Lisa Del Guidice, whose compassion and upbeat personality brought some light-hearted moments into the rehabilitation process at the Rusk Institute.

Dr. Fred Epstein, whose brilliance was equally matched by his compassion and optimism. Dr. Fred, as he preferred to be called, never gave up on Daniel. Although he passed away in 2006, his legacy lives on and was hopefully brought to life in this book through communications with his wife, Kathy Epstein; his medical colleagues; and the baseball legend Tommy John, whose son Travis was treated by Fred. We are deeply grateful to our friend, the documentarian Ruth Thomas Suh, for sharing the extensive video interviews she conducted with Dr. Fred for her 1999 piece about Daniel and our family, entitled "Where Faith Meets Science."

Jennifer Freiman Bender, who encouraged Daniel to express himself and keep taking on the next challenge.

Teddy Frischling, who has been a close and loyal friend over the years and was one of the first responders to Daniel when he collapsed on the basketball court on that March day.

Colette Goodman, who saw Daniel's potential while he attended the BOCES program, and encouraged him to keep pushing ahead and expressing himself.

Susan Guzzardo Ronan, who worked tirelessly and creatively with Daniel in physical therapy at Rusk, urging him to give his all every day and take that very first step.

Stephanie Jensen-Moulton, who encouraged, supported and went the extra yard with Daniel at Hunter College and helped spark our family's "aha" moment.

Monsignor Dennis Keane and Father Arthur Leone for their constant prayers and support, and for their leadership in bringing our church community together to pray for Daniel when we needed them the most.

The Kefalidis family, whose friendship and consistent, constant caring and support throughout the years is something we value beyond measure.

John Mara, who showed his character, compassion and generosity by staying involved with both Daniel and DMF throughout the years.

Judy Marchese, whose love and support has meant so much to us. Thank you, Judy, for your presence, and for recalling and remembering several of Daniel's milestones at Beth Israel and Rusk.

Tamar Martin, who, like Dr. Fred, never gave up on Daniel and always believed that he would surprise many and exceed all expectations.

John Olerud, who connected with Daniel during a New York Mets community service visit to the Rusk Institute in 1997, and has remained supportive of him ever since.

Kate Parkin, whose hope was unfaltering. Kate led the physical therapy team at Beth Israel Hospital and showed remarkable dedication in helping Daniel complete the NYC Marathon in 2007.

Steve and Debbie Postler, and John and Paula Trush, for their love and compassion, and for being there for us when we needed them. They define everything that is best in family with unassuming humility. Their ability to lighten the most difficult moments with humorous banter has always been appreciated.

Dr. David Salsberg, who oversaw Daniel's cognitive recovery at the Rusk Institute and has stayed involved with our family all these many years.

Lydia Spinelli, whose kindness and understanding were constants throughout Daniel's hospitalization and continued in the years following his discharge.

Chan Suh and the aforementioned Ruth Thomas Suh, whose wisdom, concern and friendship has been a steady force in our lives.

Jason Zillo, Michael Margolis, Jason Latimer, Alexandra Trochanowski, Kenny Leandry, Dolores Hernandez, Lauren Moran, and the whole New York Yankees organization, who selected Daniel's Music Foundation for Yankees HOPE week and made July 25, 2011 such a memorable and enjoyable day. We would be remiss here not to mention Jennifer Steinbrenner Swindal, whose personal warmth and solicitude has made us feel like true members of the Yankees family.

All our friends at DMF, who were generous in sharing their experiences and recollections: Brooke Bryant, Artie Elefant (who never stopped pulling Jerome into the mix), John Marino, Nadine McNeil, Stewart Meadowcroft, Jaime Palmer, Gerry Powers, Carla Sullivan and Stanley Zucker, among others. We appreciate all that you do in helping make DMF a special place for our members.

We would also like to thank the following organizations, institutions and groups of people:

Our family, extended family and friends, who stood by us throughout the period detailed in the book and continue to do so today. Their love, dedication, thoughtfulness during all the informal gatherings in the hospital and after discharge are something we cherish and will always remember.

All the parishioners in our church, and all the people around the world, who prayed for Daniel and our family throughout the years. Your faith, good wishes and positive intentions strengthened our family's faith and helped us press on.

The medical, rehabilitative and therapeutic teams who never quit on Daniel despite his critical condition and grim prognosis. Your professionalism and extraordinary care, and willingness to go the extra mile, helped Daniel surpass all medical expectations and become the special man he is today.

The educational institutions that Daniel attended in the years after his discharge from Rusk and their staffs, including his home school teacher Lisa Cassuto; the BOCES Program, the Smith School, and Hunter College, who not only gave Daniel an extraordinary education but also allowed him to flourish and learn new skills.

The Dalton School, which has provided outstanding and continuous support and generosity before Daniel's injury and during the various stages of our family's journey afterward—Offroad, Miracles on 34th Street, the Quiet Time, and of course now at DMF. Thank You!

Our friends and peers at Agency.com and The Brick Church School, who supported our family and made extraordinary accommodations to our schedules, helping us to restore some normalcy—whatever that is—to our lives.

The people from Achilles International, who encouraged Daniel to go the extra mile. You helped show us that what sometimes seems impossible is possible.

The New York Road Runners organization for accommodating Athletes With Disabilities (AWD) at the NYC Marathon and other races and allowing Daniel and others to go beyond perceived limits.

The board, sponsors, instructors, volunteers and partners who make DMF such a special and joyful place and bring out the best in our members. A heartfelt and special thank-you to each one of you, and to ALL the members. We look forward to many more years together—and high readings on the Smile-o-meter!

We would also like to express our appreciation to Tony Lyons, president of Skyhorse Publishing, for enthusiastically taking on this book. Thank you, too, Oleg Lyubner, and Lauren Burnstein for spreading the word.

A special nod goes to our wonderful editor, Kristin Kulsavage, for her patience, forbearance, and professionalism, and for her understanding of the tremendous effort that it took to bring everything together.

Thanks to John Talbot, our agent, who worked diligently and strategically in finding the right publisher for our book.

Finally, and from our hearts, we would like to thank Jerome Preisler for his superb writing. His attention to detail and investigative nature helped uncover many facts that were previously unknown to us as a family. His patience in developing the story, researching information, and meeting and speaking to numerous people throughout the process was greatly appreciated. He made our story his story and got to know each of us intimately. We would be remiss not to mention his wife Suzanne, who we spoke with, along with Jerome, for many hours during the writing of this book.

In 2010, Daniel and Gerry Powers collaborated on an original musical composition called "Daniel's Thank You Song." We present its lyrics on the following pages and dedicate it to everyone who helped and supported us along the way.

—Nancy and Ken Trush

DANIEL'S THANK YOU SONG

For giving me my life back,
And helping me with the things I lack,
For answering all of my prayers,
And showing me the people that really care.

Thank you.

For the patient, gentle giant, my Dad,
Who's always there for me when I'm feeling bad.
For the loving, caring angel, my mother,
Who's always there for me like no other.

Thank you. Thank you.

Bridge:

For the people that helped me heal,
For their love and keeping it real,

Who know when I'm good or need to rest
Whose care and affection are the best.

Thank you for these people filled with love
Positively sent from above
Because of you my life is restored

Thank You, Thank You, Thank You, Lord.

For the guy with the big-hearted smile,
Whose kindness always radiates for miles,
Helped me learn to talk even when I couldn't walk,
For my big little brother, that generous guy.

Thank you.

For the cards, the calls, the visits and letters
For making me feel so much better
Thank you all for being there
But most importantly for all your prayer.

Bridge (repeat)

A Note from Nancy and Ken Trush

This is the story of our family's off-road journey from March 9, 1997, onward. It is one of thousands of stories about people facing adversity and near tragedy, no better and no worse than anyone else's. If we have the good fortune to live long enough in this world and compare notes, we will probably find many similarities among all of us. But the sudden, unexpected events of that day, and the days, weeks and years that followed, would put our faith, resolve and view of life to the test.

It had been an average Sunday for our family up until our oldest son Daniel, collapsed on the basketball court and we learned that one of five undetected aneurysms had burst in his head. He and his younger brother Michael were typical boys—spirited, athletic, happy. As their parents, we had a simple view of life, and had been infused with a middle-class work ethic—the idea that if you worked hard, good things would happen. We'd also been instilled with the sense that success wasn't necessarily defined by the material things you accumulated. We felt making a positive difference in other people's lives was of utmost importance. We believe that now more than ever.

This book isn't meant to offer any specific magical steps or solutions for those who may find themselves in comparable situations. It isn't intended to be a guidebook. It's just the story of what our family, friends and extended community did in *our* situation. Overall, it was written on the premise that prayer, faith, family, friends, love, compassion, acceptance and trying your hardest every day are good things. The things that help us all get through, whether we're faced with traumatic events or routine problems.

Ultimately, what happened to Daniel led our family to found *Daniel's Music Foundation,* a non-profit organization that provides free music programs for individuals with developmental and physical disabilities. It's something we could have never imagined doing before Daniel's injury. But it has brought us all tremendous fulfillment and satisfaction. We see firsthand how music and our family's core values can make a difference. Our foundation is built on the principles of respect, kindness and acceptance, and the belief that music can get through to someone when other things may not.

Please know that a portion of all proceeds that our family and the author receive from the sale of this book will be donated to DMF. If you would like to learn more about the foundation go to www.danielsmusic.org. Or if you would like to get in touch with our family, please email us at info@danielsmusic.org.

From all of us to you—we wish you peace and success in your own personal journey. Happy reading!

With gratitude,

Nancy and Ken Trush

PART ONE

OFF-ROAD

OFF-ROAD

Ken Trush stared at the machines around his son's hospital bed, listening to the cold, repetitive beeping of their monitors. The doctors had put Daniel in a medically induced coma and done a tracheotomy to ventilate him, pushing air into his lungs. He had sixteen lines connected to his body and two drains in his head, more lines running from the IV stands and life support equipment than birthdays behind him.

Ken had slept in the ICU for over a week, keeping a nightly vigil from Danny's bedside. His wife, Nancy, would be at the hospital all day and then head home every evening to take care of their younger son.

They had been told that Danny's chances were less than slim. Days earlier their parish priest, Father Keane, had rushed to the hospital and administered the sacrament of Last Rites to the twelve-year-old, tears in his eyes as he recited the prayers. Danny had incredibly hung on since, but his bleak prognosis had not improved.

Ken had never imagined this happening to his oldest child—it just seemed inconceivable. But when Daniel collapsed on the basketball court, staggering into his arms, he'd realized life could change in a heartbeat for children, their parents, and an entire family.

Ken sat there waiting, watching, and praying for a life-saving miracle. He often spoke to Daniel in a quiet voice, telling him about his day, about whatever was on the room's television set, about anything that might come to mind. Lately he'd been playing music to break the silence, hoping Danny could hear it. They had always shared a love of music, and as the days and hours had piled up, each a slow eternity punctuated only by the sound of the machines, Ken had brought a boom box to the hospital and set it at the twelve-year-old's bedside. The album he played the most was by Gloria Estefan. He hoped the melodies would soothe Danny, reach deep inside his motionless body to a part of him that remained aware of his surroundings . . . and there was another reason besides.

Ken had never found it easy to express his feelings. He could only say *I love you* so many times before the words began to seem inadequate, leaving far too much undeclared. But two songs on the disk had tapped into his emotions, and he'd played them over and over, mouthing the lyrics as if they were mantras. The ballad "Reach" spoke to him of strength and reaching beyond what one thinks he ordinarily might accomplish. Although the song he was listening to now, "I'm Not Giving You Up," was outwardly about a relationship between a man and a woman, he saw a different shade of meaning in it . . . a poignant message of unconditional love and enduring commitment that went beyond its romantic themes. It lifted his spirits and strengthened his resolve, and he hoped it would do the same for Danny.

Gently now, softly, Ken began singing to the music. He wanted his son to know he would be there for him, and would go the distance, regardless of where his journey might lead. But Daniel showed no sign of hearing him. His eyes shut, his body motionless, he was unresponsive as the life support equipment continued to sustain his vital functions, its rhythmical beeps and pulses delivering a grim, insistent message of their own.

CHAPTER ONE

Two Weeks Earlier

*T*wo Weeks Earlier Sunday started out picture perfect. It was mild for early March, a morning washed with brilliant sunshine, the air clear, crisp, and invigorating as Ken took his regular jog through Central Park. He loved the areas circling the reservoir for their tranquility, the quiet, tree-lined stillness helping him stay centered amid his fast-paced professional routine. He also thought of the park as New York's great social equalizer. You could pass a millionaire celebrity or an hourly wage worker and never know the difference. People were people. What they did for a living and the amount they earned didn't deter them from sharing the same paths. Something about that deeply appealed to him, though he might not have been able to explain why.

A tall, lean, athletic man in his early forties, Ken was doing quite well in his own career. His successful financial consultancy handled accounting and tax work for about ten privately held companies, among them Agency.com, an aggressive pioneer in the field of website development and online marketing. On the verge of an international expansion, its founders, Chan Suh and Kyle Shannon, had come to rely heavily on his input, effectively making him their outsourced chief financial officer.

Dedicated to advancing Agency's corporate growth, Ken had recently traveled to London to work on an overseas deal—his first trip abroad, and one that had by turns induced excitement and nervousness. But his first priority was his family, and he'd reserved this weekend for them. Though they had been out late attending a bar mitzvah in New Jersey, the Trushes were looking ahead to a full, active day together. Around noon, Ken and Nancy were bringing their younger son, Michael, along to Danny's basketball clinic at The Dalton School Physical Education Center, on East 89th Street where they would cheer from the sidelines as usual. Next up was lunch at McDonald's; the restaurant was holding a Monopoly game promotion, and the boys were eager to collect its advertised giveaways. Finally, Ken, Danny, and Michael could hardly wait to watch that evening's big New York Knicks game on television.

Mostly because of the game, Danny's coach, Teddy Frischling, would always remember the date: March 9, 1997. This was the year after Michael Jordan led the Chicago Bulls to a playoff victory over the Knicks, and the Bulls were in town for a feverishly hyped matchup at Madison Square Garden. Teddy would also recall that he'd made dinner reservations for his mom and himself at the Lenox Room, a posh Upper Eastside restaurant where he was taking her to celebrate her birthday. He had anticipated checking the game score often throughout their meal, but it would turn out to be the last thing on his mind.

Frischling had founded his hoops program two years before and called it Dribbl, an acronym for the Dalton recreational instructional basketball league. The athletic director at Dalton, he'd separated the program from the prep school's auspices shortly after getting it off the ground. Through a special arrangement with the school, however, he continued to use the gym facilities a couple of blocks south of the main building, teaching neighborhood boys and girls fundamentals of the game and good sportsmanship, holding weekend sessions there for different age groups.

Daniel Trush was one of Frischling's seventh-grade students at Dalton, and also one of his Dribbl kids. A lively, rail-thin boy of twelve with eyes that matched the color of his tussled, dark brown hair, he was outgoing, curious, and as quick to laugh at a joke as tell one. Besides sharing his father's love of hoops—Ken had started on the junior varsity team at UConn and also played varsity at Baruch for two years—Danny had a strong affinity for music and played a couple of instruments. Guitar was one, trumpet the other. While far from a basketball prodigy, he was a decent, enthusiastic athlete who worked hard in the gym and was receptive to instruction.

Danny had stayed home from school a few times the week before Sunday's Dribbl session. Frischling knew he'd been under the weather, but he wasn't sure what was wrong with him nor had the slightest premonition that it might be serious. From what he'd heard it was a cold, a headache, something of that nature. As a teacher, you got used to kids catching minor bugs. They came on in a hurry, lingered briefly, and passed without much ado.

In fact, Danny had started experiencing headaches of varying severity in early February. These bouts would usually occur in the morning and then again around bedtime. Soon after their onset, Ken and Nancy had grown concerned enough to make two or three separate appointments with his pediatrician, hoping to find out what was wrong. The doctor had given him blood tests and basic neurological exams, but nothing out of the ordinary turned up. A mild virus might have been the culprit, he suggested. That could sometimes bring on migraines. Thinking stress another possible cause, he asked Danny's parents whether the boy was under any unusual school or family pressures.

The Trushes had told him they didn't think so. He didn't seem nervous or troubled to them. The headaches aside, he was as upbeat and engaged as ever. They'd always striven to provide a calm, supportive home environment for the boys, with open lines of communication. They felt sure they would have known if Danny had something out of the ordinary weighing on him.

Ken and Nancy had held Danny out of class for a few days after his doctor's visit, wanting to keep close tabs on him. During that period, the headaches had subsided, and Ken and Nancy had grown optimistic that he was just about over them. He'd gone to a few recent birthday and bar mitzvah celebrations that had kept him up late, maybe spent too much time with his video games. His parents suspected these things could have combined to leave him a bit fatigued.

By late February, Danny felt well enough to resume his regular class schedule. His condition so dramatically improved, in fact, that Ken was comfortable traveling to England for a round of business meetings.

But Danny's symptoms were about to recur with a vengeance. On Saturday, Ken called Nancy from London to check in with her before his scheduled flight home. Her voice was distressed over the phone. Daniel had a headache and fever again, she told him. He'd also been very nauseous; his stomach couldn't hold anything down. Ken tried to be reassuring, but he was anxious about his son the whole time he was in the air.

When he arrived home after 11 p.m., Danny was worse, and his soaring temperature prompted his parents to alert his pediatrician by phone. He agreed to see Daniel in the morning, recommending they give him a Tylenol and keep an eye on him overnight. Hopefully he would feel better after some bed rest.

Ken took the doctor's advice. That night Daniel climbed into bed with him while Nancy joined Mike in the boys' room.

Danny slept fitfully beside Ken, running a constant fever, getting sicker as the hours wore on. Then before Sunday had dawned, he awoke with an unbearable pain between his temples.

"My head feels like it's going to explode," he groaned.

Ken would later say these were the keywords for him and Nancy, the words that decided things. They had held off long enough.

They quickly got Danny dressed, Ken calling the pediatrician at home to inform him that he was bringing his son to the hospital. It was now about three o'clock in the morning, and the doctor, roused out of bed, agreed the boy had to be examined without delay. The Trushes were not ones to panic.

With Nancy staying behind to watch their younger son, Ken hurried out into the cold twilight, carrying Danny half a block from the building entrance to flag down an empty cab. The nearest ER was almost a mile south of their apartment and Daniel was in agony.

"We're heading to Lenox Hill Hospital," Ken told the driver. "The emergency room."

Traffic was sparse at that hour, and they were at the hospital in minutes. The triage nurse gave Danny a mild analgesic to swallow and instructed that they sit in the waiting room until the doctor on call was ready for them.

They spent almost two hours in the room's hard plastic chairs. When he finally saw the doctor, Danny had begun to feel better, but Ken reminded him to describe the excruciating pain he'd been in after waking up. That prompted the doctor to give him essentially the same neurological exam he'd gotten from his pediatrician back in February—routine tests for strength, reflexes, gait, eye movement, visual range and acuity, and other indications of a brain disorder. Again, the boy's results were fine. The doctor concurred with the pediatrician's assessment that his symptoms were probably common migraines, and sent Danny and his father on their way.

It was almost seven o'clock in the morning when they got back home. Danny still had a lingering headache, but it continued to fade throughout the day. As a precaution, Ken and Nancy phoned his pediatrician to ask for a referral to a neurologist, picked up the authorization early that week, and were able to make an appointment for the following Tuesday. In the section of the form he filled out to explain Danny's problem to the consulting physician, the pediatrician simply jotted: *Migraine headaches?*

His appointment still a full week off, Daniel returned to school Wednesday and seemed entirely recovered from whatever had been ailing him. Teddy Frischling thought he seemed pretty normal in gym class. Frischling had a shootaround drill in which he picked three boys from the group at random to take shots from different areas on the court. It was a fun exercise for them, and the reward if all three hit their shots was that the entire group could skip instruction and play a game right away.

The first two boys succeeded, with Danny up last for the decisive shot from the top of the key.

He stepped to the line. A bounce, another, and then he set his feet and . . . *swoosh*. It fell in. That sealed it for the boys.

Game time. But not before they had a chance to swarm Danny as if he was a conquering hero, hike him up onto their shoulders, and carry him around the court. It was something else Teddy Frischling never forgot about that week.

With Daniel feeling fine Saturday, the Trushes went to the bar mitzvah at the Jersey Shore, hopping aboard a charter bus that took them to and from the affair. There was a video arcade next to the reception hall, and when Danny went in to play some games with his friends, Ken noticed that he was having a blast. He seemed back to his energetic, wisecracking self.

The following day Danny was back at the Dalton Phys. Ed. Center for Dribbl. Still in its infancy, the program didn't have a huge enrollment, and the 26-year-old Frischling and fellow coach Doug Feinberg were in the fifth-floor gym with no more than ten boys, the kids playing full court across its width, using two baskets NBA-style.

Ken, Nancy, and Michael were on the first level of the bleachers, facing one of the baskets as the game entered its fourth quarter. They felt good watching Danny have so much fun; it was a reassurance after his recent bouts of illness. He was hustling across the court with the ball and seemed completely back to normal, showing no sign of pain, fatigue, or discomfort.

Then in a heartbeat, everything changed. With Frischling watching from midcourt, Danny took a jump shot from the left side of the key and missed. As the ball rebounded, he threw his hands up to his head and held it between them.

Ken's first thought was that his son was upset about the missed basket . . . which didn't make much sense. Danny wasn't temperamental and had never carried on about that sort of thing. But Ken only had a moment to process what was happening. He would never be able to adequately describe his feeling of dreamlike unreality as Danny turned to face him, still holding his temples. Never remember coming down off the bleachers to meet him on the court. Just Danny running toward him with his hands to his head as if to prevent it from blowing to pieces.

Then Danny slumped into his arms.

"Teddy!" Ken was screaming his name from the sideline. "Teddy, *come here!*"

Frischling bolted across the court. Meanwhile, Nancy and Michael had already reached Danny. Out the corner of his eye, Mike noticed some of the other kids still shooting around on the other side of the gym and instantly got upset at them. What were they doing over by the baskets? Why hadn't the game come to a halt? Danny was his idol. Though he sometimes gave Mike a hard time like any big brother, he was always the first one to stand up for him when he needed it. Now he was sprawled out on the floor, helpless. Didn't those kids realize what was going on?

Of course Michael had focused on his brother from the sideline their heads in the game, the other boys just thought he'd taken a spill.

Glancing down at Danny as Ken eased his limp form to the floor, Frischling made no such mistake. The boy had lost consciousness in his father's arms, retching, his right leg spasming. He was having some kind of seizure.

As a teacher, Frischling had seen kids in his classes get dizzy or pass out from hyperventilation, fevers, and even allergic reactions. Usually the underlying conditions were minor, and the kids came to without serious consequence. Yet Frischling thought this seemed different, more severe.

After a moment Danny threw up, and Frischling's worries increased. Turning to Ken and Nancy, he realized they were afraid Danny might choke on his vomit. In the confusion, he didn't know whether they said something about it or if it came across from their expressions and body language.

"As long as you angle his head so he doesn't swallow, he'll be okay," he said, trying to reassure himself as much as Ken and Nancy.

One of them turned Daniel's head sideways. His mind flashing to CPR techniques he'd learned in a course for teachers, Frischling sent Feinberg to call an ambulance from his third floor office. Ken also rushed down to it, barely aware of the assistant coach, hastening in ahead of him to grab the telephone and frantically dial 911.

Upstairs with Daniel, Frischling continued to mentally replay the resuscitation procedures he'd practiced in his yearly refresher sessions. He'd never applied them in a real-life emergency and prayed he would get them right if they were necessary.

He was spared ever having to find out. An emergency services vehicle arrived within a few short minutes, the technicians racing over to where Danny lay sprawled on the hardwood. Slowly, carefully, they lifted him onto a gurney. With Frischling and the Trushes watching, they took his baseline vitals.

"I think it's the left side of his brain," Frischling told them. He was fighting to stay composed, his tongue stumbling over the words. "His right side . . ."

Frischling might or might not have let the sentence trail, he wasn't sure, and didn't even know for certain what had prompted it. He still hadn't grasped the seriousness of Danny's condition. But he knew the brain's left hemisphere generally controlled motor functions on the right side of the body, where Danny's leg was having spasms. It was information he'd wanted to share with the techs.

His parents and brother at his side, Danny was wheeled out through a hallway into an elevator and down to the waiting ambulance. As it sped toward Lenox Hill—the same hospital Ken had brought him to the previous week—he seemed to be coming around, and one of the EMTs started asking him a series of hurried questions to test his level of awareness. What day was it? What had he been doing at the gym? How did he feel?

Danny gave the correct answers and explained that he had an intense, throbbing pain in his head. His lucid responses gave Ken a small spark of hope that he was returning to normal . . . that this latest episode would pass like the others.

Ten minutes after leaving Dalton, the ambulance screamed up to the Lenox Hill emergency room's entrance, and Danny was rushed inside to triage. His head was still hurting badly, but he remained coherent and aware of his surroundings.

Things would change for the worse in a heartbeat. As one of the doctors took a blood sample from Daniel's right arm, his eyes rolled into his head and sunk deep into their sockets. Then he started to convulse again. Ken was overcome with renewed horror and disbelief. They were losing Danny; he could see the life being sucked out of him by whatever was causing his seizures.

In a daze, Ken and Nancy were hustled outside by several nurses, more doctors and aides pouring into the room amid overlapping shouts of "STAT!" Three of them converged around Danny, working to save his life.

None of it could be happening, Ken thought. Except it was.

Peering into the triage area, he saw Danny's paroxysms suddenly stop. He'd either lapsed back into unconsciousness or been sedated. Meanwhile the on-call pediatrician, Dr. Erika

Landau, was adamant that Danny be transferred to the Beth Israel Medical Center North Division uptown, not far from the Trushes' apartment. The center housed the Hyman-Newman Institute for Neurology and Neurosurgery, or INN, founded by the renowned pediatric expert Dr. Fred Epstein. His group of specialists, Landau said, would be best qualified to diagnose and treat whatever was going on with Danny.

The ER team agreed with the Romanian-born pediatrician but decided to take a CT scan of Danny's brain before putting him on an ambulance. Realizing she couldn't keep Mike, who was only nine, waiting there at the hospital, Nancy called her mother Eva to pick him up as she and Ken helplessly stood by for the scan results.

The rest was a blur for them. The ER team had initially suspected a brain tumor. But the CT scan showed significant hemorrhaging, and their preliminary opinion was revised to what they termed an AVM—an arteriovenous malformation that involved an abnormal tangle of arteries and veins. The Trushes were told these congenital defects might in rare cases lead to bleeding lesions.

The arcane medical language was too much for Ken and Nancy to process. They were reeling, fearful, overloaded with information. It was too much to absorb in a very short time.

At 6:30 p.m., Danny left Lenox Hill in the back of a howling ambulance, accompanied by his parents and Dr. Landau. When they reached Beth Israel's ER, the administrator started going through a routine check-in process, asking Ken and Nancy for their son's name, address, insurance provider, and other information. But Dr. Landau impatiently cut her short.

"This is an emergency," she insisted. "We need to go right upstairs!"

Bypassing the red tape, they were rushed into an elevator to the tenth-floor pediatric intensive care unit and promptly met in a hallway by Dr. Rick Abbott, the attending physician and Epstein's right-hand man. He knew at once that Danny's condition was dire. The boy had been unresponsive since the doctors at Lenox Hill had taken their blood sample, and his examination of the scans revealed bleeding on a devastating scale. There had been massive hemorrhaging as well as evidence of severe hematomas, or blood clots, in and around the brain. Sharing a suspicion with the doctors at Lenox, Abbott thought it might be an AVM, but a conclusive diagnosis would require further tests. Danny's condition had to be stabilized before anything else was done for him.

He was immediately brought into intensive care and hooked up to monitors and life-support equipment. In the morning, the rest of Epstein's team would arrive to conduct a series of thorough examinations.

Ken and Nancy prepared for a long, grueling night at the hospital. But first they needed to make some urgent calls and briefly headed a few blocks uptown to their apartment to use the telephone. Besides contacting family members and Father Keane, their parish priest, to inform them of Danny's situation, Ken called Fred Epstein at his Connecticut home. Although Ken had gotten the number from someone at the hospital's staff, it was listed in the public directory, a rarity among doctors of Epstein's prominence, let alone the chief of a busy hospital unit with patients from all across the country—and around the world. That was entirely in character for him, however. At the INN, Epstein had fostered an open, humane atmosphere that broke down the barriers between healer and patient. His accessibility was part of it.

Projecting extraordinary warmth, compassion, and honesty over the phone, Epstein explained that he'd already been informed of Danny's case, assured Ken his son was in the best of hands, and told him that he would be at Beth Israel in the morning to examine the various test results. Ken found himself heartened by his supportive tone.

With their series of calls completed, and Mike in Grandma Eva's dependable care, Ken and Nancy returned to Beth Israel. The INN had a parents' lounge with comfortable reclining chairs, and Nancy's sister Debbie joined them overnight. Now there was nothing left to do but wait and pray.

The Trushes had always had strong spiritual beliefs, and now they would turn to them for comfort and strength. Devout Catholics, they formed an immediate bond with Rabbi Mychal Springer, the hospital's founding chaplain. Another component of Epstein's philosophy toward treating the sick was a respect for all religions, and the ward's young patients, families, and medical caregivers could gather regularly in the rabbi's inter-denominational services and prayer circles. Springer made the Trushes feel she understood what they were going through, what they were *feeling*. More important, perhaps, she offered hope that things would somehow work out.

The long night wore on, Nancy, Ken, and Debbie snatching what little sleep they could in the lounge. Ken periodically got up and went to the ICU to check on Danny, who remained unconscious. In soft, comforting tones, Ken would tell him that he was in good hands and that his family was close by. Once Ken thought he saw Danny move his big toe and grew hopeful he'd heard and understood him. Partly for that reason, and partly because of the confidence Epstein and his team instilled, Ken had a sense that everything would be okay and that life would soon return to normal.

But he was wrong. The Trushes' lives would never be the same, a realization that would start to sink in the next morning, when Ken and Nancy received unexpectedly bad news from the doctors . . . news that would send their family into a long, hard journey through an unpredictable off-road landscape, putting their faith and tenacity to the extreme test.

CHAPTER TWO

The phrase Ken and Nancy were hearing was "brain aneurysm." Frightening as it sounded, its definition was vague in their minds. To their knowledge no one in their family had ever been diagnosed with an aneurysm of any type. It was something foreign and unfamiliar to them.

That would now change in the most personal way.

Dr. Alex Berenstein broke the news the morning after Danny arrived at Beth Israel. As with the rest of the INN's staff, he'd been handpicked by Fred Epstein, with whom he'd worked for years at the New York University Medical Center's famed pediatric neurosurgery unit, where Epstein had built his reputation. Born in Mexico City, Berenstein had immigrated to the United States in the 1970s and become a pioneer in the evolving field of neuroradiology. In his days at NYU, he'd developed increasingly sophisticated catheterization techniques for the treatment of brain tumors and other vascular abnormalities of the head and neck.

Berenstein's plain language and steady, upfront manner made an instantly favorable impression on the Trushes. His review of

Daniel's imaging scans—the medical team had taken an MRI with contrast—had shown that Danny had not one but *five* aneurysms in the left side of his brain, all on a single blood vessel.

Berenstein explained that an aneurysm was an abnormal dilation, or swelling, in an arterial wall. Arteries were the narrow tubes that carried blood from the heart through the rest of the body. When any portion of an artery's wall was compromised, the pressure of the blood flowing through it sometimes made that area balloon outward and rupture like an air bubble in a worn section of a tire. There was no way to be positive how long the malformations had existed, but Berenstein guessed Danny was born with them. As the weakest, thinnest segment of the arterial wall bulged further and further outward, it would have pressed against surrounding brain and nerve tissue and caused the headaches, nausea, and fever that had plagued the boy in recent weeks. It had finally burst yesterday at the gym. As with any physical activity, playing basketball would have caused a rise in blood flow through the artery, increasing the pressure inside it. That had probably put added stress on the compromised spot and ruptured it.

While no one could say for sure if Danny's exertions had been the last straw, it was a moot point. Sooner or later the vessel would have popped, and the important thing was to address what was going on in his head right now. Berenstein seconded Dr. Abbott's observation of multiple hematomas. Danny's brain had also swollen as a result of the trauma. Both the swelling and the clotting were regular biological mechanisms that occurred with bleeding injuries, but what differentiated the human skull from other parts of the body was that it was a rigid shell with little room to accommodate *either* mechanism. The resultant pressure buildup in Danny's intracranial spaces had led to his convulsions and coma. His brain had effectively signed off. Before anything could be done to get it back online, the bleeding had to be stopped and the swelling brought under control.

Ken and Nancy struggled to absorb this information. To simply make sense of it all. Just hours before, Danny had been on the basketball court looking forward to McDonald's and some family time watching a basketball game on TV. It was as if they'd been struck by a ferocious, random lightning bolt.

Berenstein, meanwhile, was resolutely straightforward with them. "Your son is very, very sick," he said. "You have a choice . . . either you let me put a platinum coil into the bleeding aneurysm or I give you the MRIs and you go to another hospital."

Another hospital? Those words left the Trushes feeling even more stunned and lost. *Where else could they take him? Were they supposed to shuttle Danny from place to place in a coma?*

Although Dr. Berenstein's bluntness presented a contrast to Epstein's gentle reassurance, the Trushes would later see it as having been necessary under the circumstances—a splash of cold water that made it clear they couldn't afford to delay taking action. Berenstein left them with no question about the severity of Daniel's condition. He'd said they had a choice, but there really wasn't one. Not for them, not for their son.

Now Berenstein hastily told the Trushes about the procedure he wanted to conduct on Danny. Known as endovascular aneurysm coiling—endovascular meant *inside* the blood vessel, where the platinum coil would be implanted—its whole purpose was to stop Danny's cerebral hemorrhage. The coil, the doctor explained, was smaller than a strand of hair. It would be introduced into the child's body through an incision in his groin with a micro catheter, then advanced up the femoral artery and into Danny's aorta, passing through his heart and up into the carotid artery. The artery's ruptured segment was located where the artery bifurcated, or forked, behind his eye.

Berenstein's confidence in the procedure had the strongest foundation one could have imagined—he had helped develop it at NYU. Persuaded by his assurances, Ken and Nancy gave their consent on the spot. The no-nonsense Berenstein didn't waste a minute getting Daniel prepped for surgery.

Again, his parents could only wait and pray. While their faith was a private matter, they were very open about its importance in their lives. Prayer and spiritual reflection were a vital, integrated part of Ken's ordinary routine. On days he ran in the park, his warm-up exercises would be accompanied by silent thanks for the blessings granted his family, for his modest personal needs, and for other people's needs.

For Ken, whose systematic mind had served him well in his career, these prayers had a particular form, a structured, meaningful order that he'd followed since his teens. He would always begin with the Our Father, believing its initial expression of devotion, followed by its humble requests for God's help and forgiveness and ultimate acceptance of His will, fully expressed the connection between man and his Maker. Then he would recite the traditional prayer to the Virgin Mary for her holiness and embracing sweetness. Only after this would he ask for divine assistance, while truly believing that God helped those who helped themselves ... that people had to try as hard as they could at whatever they hoped to accomplish, while accepting that a higher power would have the ultimate say in their success.

Ken's idea of acceptance was far from passive—you did whatever you could to achieve your goals. You always did what you could, putting yourself in the best position for good things to happen. If you made your best effort, it was easy leaving the rest to faith.

As Dr. Berenstein went to work on their son, Ken and Nancy waited in the lounge where they had spent the night, joined by family and friends, their prayers taking on newfound intensity. They were what Ken called *hard* prayers for God to give Danny strength and lend the doctors wisdom through His guidance as they turned all their medical knowledge and abilities toward fighting for Danny's survival.

Sometime that morning, Fred Epstein arrived at Beth Israel and introduced himself to the Trushes in person. With his ready smile, flyaway white hair, and designer cowboy boots, Epstein instantly reinforced the approachable and mildly unconventional impression Ken had gotten from him over the phone. He preferred to be called by his first name—the nameplate on his office door simply read FRED—but didn't object when the Trushes respectfully called him *Doctor* Fred. The forcefully positive Epstein added a crucial measure of hope and empathy to the confidence Berenstein had instilled in Ken and Nancy, who would need a mix of all three to see them through their coming trials.

Meanwhile, Berenstein's procedure had begun in a textbook manner. After being hustled into the OR, Danny was anesthetized and placed between an x-ray machine and fluoroscopic screen, allowing Berenstein to use real-time internal imagery to obtain a road map for directing the coil through the boy's vascular system into his skull, and then implanting it in the area of the burst aneurysm. Afterward the catheter would be withdrawn and the wound in his upper leg cleaned, closed, and dressed. The coil would permanently stay in place and trigger his body's clotting reaction, blocking the blood flow from the compromised vascular segment and forcing it to take another route. In time, the normal healing process would create scar tissue that would seal off the damaged blood vessel.

But things did not entirely go according to plan. While studying the fluoroscopic images, Berenstein detected a significant complication: The aneurysm had not one but *two* bubbles, although only one of them had burst. Berenstein still felt the procedure could be successfully conducted—as he had told the boy's parents, there was really no choice—but the double projections increased the challenge of manipulating the coil into its correct position.

About three hours after Danny was brought in for the procedure, Berenstein emerged from the OR. Accompanied by Epstein and Abbott, he met Ken and Nancy in the lounge and detailed how the surgery had gone.

It hadn't been easy, he said. Bringing a pen out of his pocket, he informed the Trushes of the aneurysm's uncommon shape and sketched a rough diagram of the two bubbles on the leg of his scrub pants, describing them as "Mickey Mouse ears." But despite the unexpected snag, Berenstein had finally managed to get the coil in place and stem the bleeding from the ruptured arterial wall.

Ken thought all three doctors seemed upbeat, although they cautioned that Daniel wasn't out of the woods; they had yet to control the swelling in his brain, and the following days would determine their success. He would vaguely remember them using the term ICP after the surgery. But Ken and Nancy had been bombarded with a great many terms in the past few hours, and they were too relieved the operation had gone well to pay much attention to it.

Unfortunately, they would learn that with Danny in his current state it meant nothing good.

CHAPTER THREE

Mondays were off days for Phys. Ed. classes at Dalton, giving Teddy Frischling an opportunity to walk the few blocks from his office to Beth Israel and see how Danny Trush was doing. He was concerned as hell about the kid without quite being able to fully absorb the seriousness of his condition. It had happened so fast, Danny playing basketball one moment, and the next lying there on the floor of the gymnasium in convulsions. Then before Frischling had known it, the Trushes were gone, the ambulance gone, and Danny was being sped to the hospital.

At the restaurant with his mother Sunday night, Frischling had excused himself from dinner to call the Trushes at their apartment. But nobody was home, and he'd left a brief message on their answering machine just to give his well wishes. He'd kept his fingers crossed that whatever might be wrong with Danny wasn't life threatening.

His friend Alan Mason, a senior administrator at Dalton, admittedly had not sounded very sanguine when they spoke on the phone earlier. Frischling had been Mason's student once upon a time, and they'd remained close now that Frischling had joined the teaching staff. He knew Mason also had a special bond with the Trushes but wasn't clear about how their relationship had formed.

In fact, they were linked by the friendship between Mason's son, Ben, and Danny, who were both classmates. As an assistant director at Dalton, Mason had been notified that Danny was in the hospital and gone directly there after school to visit with the boy's parents.

Before he headed over that afternoon, Frischling had called Mason to make sure his showing up wouldn't be an intrusion. On the contrary, Mason told him, Ken and Nancy were camped out in the waiting room indefinitely and would welcome his company.

At the hospital, Frischling went up to the INN and saw Mason, along with one of Danny's close friends and the Trushes, in the parents' lounge. Their expressions immediately told him that Danny's condition was graver than anything he'd imagined. He was informed about the five aneurysms in his head, and one bursting, and the doctors having to surgically implant a metal coil in a blood vessel to stop the bleeding. It was all really confusing to him; he'd never paused to think Danny might not make it. But now he had the sinking feeling it was more than possible.

Ken and Nancy held a far different view. Their relief over the success of the coiling procedure had given them a brighter attitude. They were drained but optimistic that the worst had passed for Danny.

Early that evening Nancy went back to their apartment. Ken's mother Jeanne was chipping in with Michael's care. But with Danny apparently in stable condition, Nancy wanted to spend some time with Mike and help get him ready for school the next morning. Ken planned to spend a second night at the hospital, having assured Nancy he would contact her at once if there was anything new to report.

Monday night passed without incident. Danny was unresponsive but remained in stable condition, showing no signs of discomfort. The light fixtures in the INN's parent lounge were dimmed so family members could sleep, and Ken managed to do just that between visits to his son's bedside.

Exhausted from the ordeal of the last two days, he had no idea how long he had dozed when the room suddenly brightened around him. He'd heard someone call his name, or thought he had, but in his disorientation wondered fuzzily if he might have been dreaming.

"Wake up, Mr. Trush . . . wake up. . . ."

Still out of sorts, Ken checked the time and saw that it was five o'clock in the morning. The figure of a man stood over him. After a moment, he realized it was the neurosurgeon . . . Dr. Abbott. Ken saw fatigue in his eyes—and something else. A deep, deep sadness. It made him straighten in his chair.

"Your son's gone from bad to worse," Abbott said. "He's not going to make it. Get your family to say good-bye."

Ken struggled to pull himself together as Abbott briefed him on what was going on. He again used the term ICP, the one Ken remembered hearing from the doctors after Alex Berenstein implanted the platinum coil. At the time he and Nancy had been too flushed with relief to lock in on it. Now Abbott's every word would ring clearly in his mind forever.

Daniel's intracranial pressure, or ICP, had skyrocketed to fifty, Abbott informed him. That was higher than his ordinary blood pressure, meaning higher than the pressure within the arteries trying to pump oxygenated blood up into his head. When blood couldn't get into the head and brain tissues—a process known as blood perfusion—the brain would die within five to ten minutes. Although the blood flow to Danny's brain hadn't stopped, the resistance created by the elevated ICP had severely limited it. His prognosis was bleak; the odds were that he did not have long to live.

Get your family to say good-bye.

Ken was a realistic man, inclined to assess situations objectively. One of his personal mottos was "The facts shall set you free," a take on the biblical proverb, "The truth shall set you free." But nothing could have prepared him for what Abbott had told him. He felt as if he'd been hit with a mallet.

Devastated, he hurried over to Danny's bedside. He needed time to process everything, to simply be with his son.

Ken spent the greater portion of an hour alone with him, holding his hand, smelling his hair with the thought that he might never again have the chance, wanting to imprint its scent on his memory. He prayed intensely, tears streaming from his eyes. Then he tried to get a grip on himself. Danny was running out of time. He had to go home and break the news to Nancy and Michael. But *how*? What words would he use? Mike was so young. He hadn't yet seen his brother in the hospital. Ken knew bringing him here would be traumatic . . . especially first thing in the morning, when he was barely awake and had no preparation at all for what awaited.

Before leaving for home, Ken paused to ask Dr. Abbott for advice. Should he even consider having the younger boy visit Danny in his present condition? Seeing him in a coma with drains and lines attached to him . . . what psychological scars might that leave?

Abbott was sympathetic. "I can't tell you what to do," he said. "But maybe it would be better for Michael to remember Daniel as he was."

Ken took a taxi back to his apartment. It was now almost six-thirty in the morning, the streets still dark outside, daybreak a few hours off. He sat in the cab's backseat, staring out the window, his worried mind turning toward Nancy. He didn't know how she would react to the situation. Didn't know if she'd be able to handle it. In their fifteen years of marriage, they'd never faced anything this overwhelming. The closest episode he could remember—and it wasn't really even comparable— was when Daniel was born. Nancy had experienced prolonged labor, and although it put her in tremendous pain, she never broke water. Though Ken had heard stories of women who'd had difficulty tolerating rough deliveries, Nancy had shown steady composure even when having double contractions. But the pain of childbirth was something she alone knew, and now it wasn't about *her* pain at all. This time was about Daniel, and she was like a protective lioness when it came to her children's welfare.

Ken dreaded the task awaiting him at home. He had to impress the urgency of things on his family while trying not to send them into a panic. Then he needed to get Nancy over to the hospital. His mother had stayed the night, and he'd already asked her to bring Michael to school. Without having gotten a chance to speak to him about Danny, Ken couldn't imagine having him see his older brother in his present state. Better to take Abbott's advice and spare him that shattering experience.

Tearing free of his thoughts, Ken exited the cab and then hurried through his building's lobby to the elevators. *Nancy to the hospital, Mike to school.* The plan was simple yet daunting.

The instant he walked through the door, Ken saw that everyone was awake. That surprised him. The last Nancy had heard at the hospital was Dr. Berenstein's comment that the coiling procedure had gone well. As far as she knew, there had been no further updates from the medical team. Preoccupied as he'd been since Abbott roused him with his bad news, Ken hadn't considered that his family might be sleepless with more general anxieties about Daniel.

Finding all of them out of bed did more than take him aback—it forced a quick decision. He would say as little as possible in front of Mike. Nancy would realize that whatever had brought him back to the apartment must be serious. She wouldn't need details on the spot, and he wouldn't give them to her. It would spare the nine-year-old from hearing anything he couldn't handle.

"The doctors want to see us," Ken said simply. Then he fell silent, not wanting to trigger alarms.

It might have been the look on his face, but those few words were enough. Nancy asked no questions. Instead she helped Mike get dressed for school, threw on her coat, gave him and Grandma Jeanne hugs and kisses good-bye, and left with Ken for Beth Israel.

For Ken it was the second uneasy cab ride in an hour. When Nancy finally pressed for more information, he just repeated that the doctors had asked to speak to them. Mostly he sat beside her with trepidation, thinking about Daniel, wondering if he'd even be alive when they reached the hospital. The fear that he wouldn't had taken stubborn hold of his mind, and it was growing stronger as they neared their destination.

By the time they passed through the sliding doors at Beth Israel, Ken was overcome with worry. His legs were numb and weak, and everything around him seemed faraway, almost part of another world. He'd only felt that way once or twice before— most hauntingly when he was twenty-one and his father Nick suffered a pulmonary embolism. He would forever recall the date as December 25, 1976. Christmas Day. The family had been going to church in a taxi when Nick Trush passed out in his seat, and the driver sped them over to the nearest emergency room. By the time they arrived, Nick had regained conscious- ness, but he went into cardiac arrest as he was leaving the car. The medical personnel immediately appeared in the parking lot, laid him out on the ground, and started CPR.

Ken carried a lasting image of them ripping off Nick's coat on the asphalt and doing a chest compression, using the pads to shock his heart into rhythm. Then they put him on a stretcher or gurney and brought him straight into the emergency room. Ken had felt like he wasn't quite there; everything seemed slow and illusory.

It was eerily similar for him now. He might have been walking through a movie that was spooling out in slow motion . . . except it was all really happening. He expected the worst and couldn't rid himself of the sense that he and Nancy were too late. That Danny had died and they would find his room empty, or see him lying in bed with a white sheet pulled up over his face, the life-support equipment disconnected and silent.

When they got up to the ICU, Ken almost couldn't believe his eyes. Danny was in his bed, still on the lines. Still *alive*.

He and Nancy sank into chairs and waited for the doctors. Soon Dr. Abbott came in to tell them of some new developments.

"Daniel autoregulated," he said. His tone was positive but restrained. "He brought up his blood pressure himself."

The Trushes were confused. Again they were struggling to absorb information about something light years beyond their experience. How could Danny have done it on his own? They listened carefully as Abbott explained.

Blood vessels in the brain had a certain natural elasticity. Under ordinary circumstances, if a person's blood pressure went down, the arteries transporting blood from the heart to the brain expanded to allow a greater cerebral flow. If the blood pressure increased, the vessels constricted so too much blood wasn't being shot into the brain.

Danny's situation was anything but ordinary, however. The high pressure in the fluid spaces of his brain had been closing off the blood flow from the heart. His circulatory system had then compensated by raising his blood pressure enough to keep the flow going up to his head.

Despite this reprieve, Abbott advised the Trushes to keep their expectations in check. Danny's intracranial pressure was still dangerously elevated. Unless it leveled off, the body's internal mechanisms would eventually fail to compensate, and his brain would be ravaged until it could no longer sustain even his basic vital functions.

But Ken and Nancy had seized on a thread of hope. Danny's self-regulation told them he was fighting. He was somewhere inside his comatose body, doing everything he could to survive. And if Danny was struggling that hard in the depths of his coma, how could they, as his parents, fail to equal his determination?

Ken was suddenly prepared for battle. Come what may, he decided he'd be fully engaged in the efforts to save Danny, involved with every aspect of his care, ready to face any obstacles that might arise. While he believed in the ability of Danny's doctors, and trusted them to do their best, he would help and support them in any way possible. While he believed God had a plan for everyone, and trusted in *it*, he also believed it was incumbent on human beings to do everything they could to help themselves. As long as Danny was alive, he would stand behind him. He understood that he was just at the beginning of what was likely to be a long war, but his faith and trust allowed him to accept any outcome.

Ken would come to feel that moment changed him forever. It went beyond his newfound resolve; his perception of Nancy had changed as well. Everyone who knew his wife—their friends, relatives, and her colleagues at The Brick Church School, where she taught three-year-olds in the morning and older children in the afternoon—was familiar with her warmth and modest sincerity. Ken had always seen her as the gentlest, most loving person he had ever met, someone who never failed to put her family's needs before her own. But he'd equated her gentleness with a lack of strength—and the quiet poise and dignity with which she'd handled the morning's events had revealed that to be a mistake. She was as ready to fight for Danny as he was.

Ken knew he would not have to be overprotective of her going forward. She could hear anything, and handle anything, without him acting as a buffer. Her poise and courage were a revelation, a liberating discovery that raised their level of communication and deepened their marital relationship. Her hidden strength had also taught him about the danger of judging others based on premature assumptions. In the future he would let people's actions speak for them, reserve his judgments, and take the time to carefully evaluate what they presented to him—what *life* presented—before forming opinions and conclusions.

Later that morning, Ken and Nancy sat down to talk as husband and wife, as Daniel's parents, as *one*. Their open, unfiltered conversation led to a pact of sorts: They pledged that they were going to be true and equal partners in his care, "a team without a superstar." They would make all major decisions together . . . and not just those that involved Danny.

Among the toughest questions confronting them was what to tell Mike about his older brother's condition—and when to do it. He'd been awake with Nancy and his grandmother when Ken walked into the apartment thinking Danny was near death. Although his parents had only exchanged a few words before leaving for the hospital, Mike was a sharp, perceptive kid. He had surely perceived Ken's distress and wondered why he'd come all the way home for Nancy. Thinking he must be very confused and anxious, his parents concluded it was best not to delay addressing things with him.

Shortly after Mike got home from school that afternoon, Ken took him down to a little playground alongside their apartment building. There wasn't much to it, just a jungle gym, parallel bars, and some planters. But for Ken and the boys it was the urban equivalent of a backyard, a place where they regularly came to toss around a baseball or football.

Ken stuck to routine with Mike, playing catch for a while, figuring it would impart a semblance of normalcy and relax him . . . relax *both* of them for that matter. After a while he sat down on one of the planters, hoisted Mike up onto his lap, and prepared to explain what was going on. But how *did* you tell a nine-year-old he might never see his older brother again? How could you get him ready for that?

Ken was on untrodden ground, with nothing but instinct and common sense to guide him. Deep thoughts and feelings had been rarely expressed in his own parents' home; Nick and Jeanne Trush had practiced the quiet stoicism common to a genera-tion that grew up amid the prevalent hardships of World War

Two. But he and Nancy were from a time of greater emotional openness, and they'd always kept an honest dialog with their children. Ken was determined to be truthful with Mike, while reminding himself that he was still a little boy. A boy who saw his big brother Daniel as an invincible hero.

"Danny's very sick," he began gently. "He's in a coma."

Michael's eyes grew moist. A scrawny kid with big round-framed eyeglasses, he searched his father's face, trying to draw understanding from it. "What's a coma look like?"

"It's like he's sleeping," Ken said. "His brain's injured. It has to rest and get better."

"Is Danny in pain?"

Ken chose his words with care, wanting to be as delicate as possible. Daniel appeared comfortable. It was something that had given him and Nancy a modicum of solace.

"Probably not," he said, truthfully. "But we aren't sure when he's going to wake up, or when he'll come home again."

Now tears were spilling from under Mike's glasses, leaving shiny wet tracks on his cheeks. Sitting with him perched on his thigh, Ken fought to keep his own tears at bay. It took a colossal effort.

Soon the two went upstairs, where Nancy was waiting for them. Together, Ken and Nancy did their best to comfort Mike, stressing that they would always be there for him, in every way, despite having to spend the bulk of their time at the hospital with Danny.

Although Mike seemed okay after their talk, Nancy was left feeling concerned. A hospital was a scary place for kids *and* grown-ups. But at least adults understood why their loved ones were there, saw them being cared for, got the whole picture. Mike possessed an active young imagination. What sort of strange, frightening images would it conjure? Would protecting him from the reality of his brother's situation only make things worse?

Ken had helped explain Danny's absence to Mike, and that was an important step in his adjustment. But in the back of her mind, Nancy wondered if something else might have to be done.

CHAPTER FOUR

O ver the next couple of days, Nancy couldn't shake the feeling that Mike just wasn't himself. There were subtle yet noticeable signs. He'd always been quiet—especially to people outside their immediate family—but now he was subdued even at home, around those closest to him. The questions he'd asked Ken about Danny also troubled her. *What does he look like? Is he in pain? When is he coming home?* Mike seemed to be growing more apprehensive about his brother each day Danny was gone.

When she talked it over with Ken, they agreed it would be best that he visit Danny in the hospital. He needed to see that his brother was in good hands, surrounded by doctors and nurses who were doing their best to make him well.

Ken and Nancy shared their thoughts with Dr. Edward Conway, the intensivist in charge of close monitoring and life support in the ICU. Conway's kids were fairly close to theirs in age, and he was not only sympathetic but also had an idea about how to make the visit easier for Mike. When he got to the hospital, Conway would have a kind of show-and-tell ready in his office, using an anatomical model of the human head as a prop to help explain Danny's condition. That way nothing he saw during his visit would come as a total shock.

Ken and Nancy were grateful. The doctors had inserted drainage catheters into two of Danny's cerebral ventricles—fluid-filled cavities within the brain. Normally the fluid served as a buffer against traumatic injury and a means of transporting hormones and other bodily materials to and from the brain's hemispheres. But in Danny's case there was too much fluid accumulating in those spaces, and they had become severely enlarged, which added to the swelling of his brain tissues. Unless Conway prepared Mike, his parents feared those drains would look like something out of a horror film to him. Even so they worried about how he'd react.

But they had made their decision. From the younger boy's perspective, Danny had dropped off into a total void. Nothing he saw could be scarier than the unknown.

Toward the end of the week, Ken and Nancy picked Michael up from school and brought him to Conway's office off the ICU's elevators. Then they went on to Daniel's room, leaving Mike alone with the doctor.

Conway had his neurological display ready. The scale model on his desk came apart to reveal the interior features of the skull and brain in detailed three-dimensional cross sections, and he calmly exhibited them so Mike could see the location of his brother's injury. He took his time describing precisely what the boy could expect in the ICU, and he even showed him the type of drains running from Danny's head, explaining how they were being used to ease the pressure inside it. After about twenty minutes, he was convinced Mike was prepared and walked him up the hall toward his parents.

When Mike saw Danny in his bed, everything was exactly as the doctor had described it. There were tubes, IVs, and machines all around his brother—so *many* machines. Mike craned his head this way and that to look at them, then returned his eyes to Danny. He was a little afraid, and kind of curious too. But mostly he was relieved to see him again. The one surprise was a baseball cap on his head . . . it didn't look as if he had it on right or was really even wearing it. Instead, it seemed to be kind of sitting there at an odd, crooked angle.

The cap held Mike's attention for a long moment as he stood in the doorway, not uttering a word to his parents.

Ken was no less quiet. He intently watched Mike for any sign that he was in distress, but he didn't cry or look agitated. The kid just seemed to be bravely taking in what he saw and assessing it for himself.

His parents kept the visit short. When they led Mike back out into the hall, he calmly told them that Danny hadn't looked too bad, but wondered aloud about the way the cap was perched on his head.

Ken and Nancy exchanged silent glances. They knew Conway had folded the cap to rest lightly over Danny's forehead and cover the drainage catheters running into it. Prepared or not, a child Mike's age couldn't have been expected to absorb so much at once.

Still, the visit reassured Mike, who would recall Dr. Conway's patient, attentive manner as tremendously comforting at a very uncertain time.

He came to see Daniel almost every day afterward and soon even got somewhat used to the tubes. Dr. Conway would often talk basketball with him and once even gave him a collectable figure of Damon Stoudamire, his favorite NBA player, as a gift. It meant a lot to him.

Nancy's instincts had been right. Mike's fear of the unknown, and the images it must have created in a young boy's fertile mind, had been worse than anything he'd had to face at the hospital. But neither she nor Ken could have realized that his first step into the ICU had been a dividing line for Mike. He had begun his transition from being a typical kid brother to playing a very different role within the family, one that would gradually shape the man he'd grow up to be.

The days and nights wore on for Ken and Nancy, one blending into the next. There were times when they believed everything would turn out all right, and times when they felt sapped and barely able to carry on. But although their poise was stretched to the limit, they never accepted the idea that God would turn away from them.

It helped that others around them shared their faith. Nancy's sister Diane placed a medallion of Saint Padre Pio of Pietrelcina, the beloved Italian saint credited with miraculous healings throughout the world, under Daniel's pillow. Diane's devout faith and constant prayers, along with the prayers of many others, proved uplifting for the family.

The Trushes were moved and strengthened by the INN's broad inclusiveness of their spiritual beliefs. The environment Dr. Epstein had promoted at the facility embraced medicine *and* prayer as tools for their son's care; it kept them hanging in, although they never quite knew what to realistically expect or hope for.

Daniel remained comatose, showing no response to stimuli, no facial expressions, no movement. The doctors had slipped inflatable compression sleeves over his calves to prevent blood clots and edema in his legs and had put fur-lined support boots on his feet to keep them from dropping down to the mattress. That would cause his Achilles tendons to shorten and make his rehab more difficult if he came to, they explained. The boots were lined with fur to warm his feet and cushion his heels from developing sores.

Meanwhile, Daniel's brain was still swelling, his intracranial pressure fluctuating uncontrollably. At times it soared so high that the flow of oxygen-rich blood to the organ was barely enough to keep it from a complete shutdown. His physicians concurred that he'd suffered irreversible brain damage. Ken had noticed that Danny's ventricle drains, which should have run clear if he was getting better, almost constantly were filled with red. Though he never asked the medical team about it, he felt there must have been heavy bleeding in Daniel's skull despite the platinum coil implant.

The Trushes could do little for Danny now but keep their steady watch at the hospital. Nancy spent her days there with him and returned home every evening to be with Mike. Then Ken would take over, sitting edgily in a chair that converted into a sleeper and shifting his gaze between Danny and the monitors, looking for any small sign that he was emerging from his coma or that he might be taking a sudden downturn. Both Ken and Nancy wrestled with a sense of powerlessness that sometimes maddened them as parents and made their prayers for Danny, and the hours they spent just talking softly to him from his bedside, take on heightened importance. They couldn't physically help him, so they reached deeply into their spiritual reserves to ask God for His mercy, guidance, and assistance.

Ken would need all that faith to get through his lonely overnight watches. Real sleep was impossible, but every now and then he'd try to shut his eyes and rest up a bit. He was rarely able to doze for long before the beeping of the monitors snapped him awake in the chair. It happened between five and ten times in the first few weeks and usually indicated a deadly jump in Daniel's intracranial pressure.

For some reason no one could pinpoint, his ICP always seemed to spike at night. While Danny would show no outward distress—he appeared peacefully asleep—the rapid beeps would tell Ken that something was terribly wrong *inside* his son. He became fixated on the monitor screens, watching them, praying the readings would return to acceptable levels.

But the kid was repeatedly pummeled. There was a horrible, grinding sameness to what would occur whenever Ken heard the alarms. At the front desk, the residents and nurses would be alerted by sounds and screen readings identical to those around Danny's bed. They would appear in a flash and "bag" him—use a ventilator mask and flexible handheld air chamber to squeeze oxygen into his lungs. Then they would rush him into a freight elevator with Ken in tow and shoot down ten floors to the imaging room for CAT scans.

Initially Ken would be asked to wait outside. But as the trips became more frequent, the technicians would let him sit in with them, and he'd watch the images come up onscreen. Though the techs never reviewed the scans with him, the doctors often did once Danny was brought back to intensive care. Ken soon learned to read them fairly well and was amazed how much he could learn about technically sophisticated medical concepts in a short time when they applied to his child—information he would have taken months, or even years, to grasp otherwise.

One of the earliest lessons in his rapid learning curve was that the little things often weren't so little for a patient in Danny's fragile condition. This was driven home early on, when the doctors realized his wire braces were causing glare spots on the scans. Clean, clear images were needed for them to know precisely what was going on in his brain. Any developing problems they missed because of reflections or distortions could snowball with disastrous consequences.

Little but not so little, simple but not so simple. An oxygen tube running directly down Danny's trachea had made his lips swell by irritating his mucous membranes. The doctors found it hard to move his mouth at all, let alone get at his braces. But somehow they would have to do it.

Ken and Nancy immediately consulted with their family friend and orthodontist, Dr. Margo Jaffe, who volunteered to take off the braces herself, insisting a practiced hand was required even if the patient was in good health and the removal was done under optimal circumstances—and Danny could claim neither. Convinced by her argument, they told the orthodontist to make the necessary arrangements.

With the hospital's permission, she went to work on Danny, arriving at the ICU with her full kit of probes, pliers, cutters, and cheek retractors. As both parents watched from his bedside, she leaned over him and pushed, pulled, and twisted hard yet deftly to coax the metallic bands off his teeth.

Everyone in the room smiled when she tugged the last wire from his mouth with an audible grunt of exertion. Ken thought it a remarkable effort and then was struck by the realization that something as simple on its face as removing braces could spell the difference between life and death. He would always remember the importance of paying attention to the small things afterward—not just as they applied to his son's care, but as a governing principle in all his personal and professional undertakings.

Danny's scans were accurate once the braces were removed . . . but unfortunately they weren't pretty. His brain was still swelling, and the doctors explained that his enlarged ventricles were putting increased pressure on the brain to expand outward against the skull. Large, ominous patches of white in different areas indicated pooling blood; Danny's oxygen deprivation, hemorrhaging, and escalated ICP had brought on multiple strokes. Ken was shown regions where there already had been catastrophic neural damage and told of the likely functional losses associated with their destruction. It was a dreadful checklist.

Here was right side and frontal lobe damage that would affect the logical processing of information, social responses, and memory. Here, left side damage—speech impairment. And here, damage to the optic nerve—impaired vision.

Dr. Abbott would drive in from his Westchester home at all hours of the night and fight till daybreak to restore the proper pressure and blood circulation to Danny's brain. But nothing seemed effective; he was unable to get the readings to smooth out.

Abbott soon grew heavily invested in the case, in part, he realized, because he'd found the boy's parents to be "absolute team members." They expected Daniel to eventually come home and wanted to do their part to *bring* him back to them. But while the Trushes became active participants in his treatment, and insisted on being given the information that was necessary for them to make intelligent decisions, they were careful not to get in the way of the doctors. It showed a respect for their professionalism, a recognition that everyone involved in his care shared the same goal.

Ken's client and close friend at the Internet development outfit Agency.com, Chan Suh, would witness the family's efforts to assist with Danny's treatment in his many visits to the hospital. Their respectful, supportive approach to helping the doctors do their jobs didn't surprise him; he saw it in large part as an extension of Ken's pragmatic but open-minded way of tackling problems across the board.

Chan had once been a beneficiary of that approach, albeit in a different situation. In 1995 he'd cofounded Agency.com with the entrepreneurial Kyle Shannon and operated on a shoe-string. Though the dynamic web shop had eventually grown into a multimillion-dollar corporation, Suh's visionary talents at "melting the technology and media businesses together" had not at first extended to profits and losses, and he was having trouble keeping his outfit in the black. When Ken had started on as an accounting consultant with Agency, its bookkeeping and financial reporting was a mess.

Suh was immediately impressed by Ken's honest, nonjudgmental assessment of the outfit's teetering financial status. He'd analyzed its problems and then worked up a long-term plan to put the company on solid ground and grow it to where its founders wanted it to be. Ken never second-guessed their earlier decisions; his focus was on present and future goals, never the past. Chan had appreciated and admired that forward-looking quality. He saw Ken as a steadying force, level and calm without being at all passive. And as someone who handled most things well.

Ken had kept Chan in the loop about Danny and appeared to be holding up okay under the circumstances. But whenever they spoke at the office or on the phone, Chan would be at a loss about what to say to him. Nor was he even sure what to ask. Even as his lips started forming questions like "How are you doing?" or "What did the doctors tell you today?" he would realize they were impossible to answer without repeating the same things over and over. Danny hadn't gotten any better. The medical professionals were doing everything in their power to keep him alive while constantly imparting the seriousness of his condition to Ken and Nancy.

Chan wondered how he could help them, thinking of practical ways. It seemed natural to bring food whenever he stopped at the hospital—and not only for the Trushes. Chan had been born in Seoul in the early 1960s, less than a decade after the Korean War. With poverty rampant, and medical facilities operating with insufficient manpower and resources, the families of patients were expected to shoulder many of the responsibilities handled by hospital staffers in Western countries. If you were hospitalized, your family had to bring all your food from outside and buy supplies like bandages and medicine from the dispensary with cash. As a boy, Chan had seen flourishing local economies grow with the markets that sprang up near hospitals, and he remembered a wide variety of foods being sold in them. But he'd sometimes wondered what happened to the little knots of poor people hunched around sick beds and looking down at the floor in silence because they had no food for their loved ones.

While it was far from that way at Beth Israel, Chan figured busy people like doctors and nurses wouldn't have the time to eat decent meals, let alone indulge in treats while on shift. In fact, he guessed, Ken, Nancy, and Mike were probably too distracted to be eating well themselves.

That got him thinking. He believed that sharing food strengthened human ties at a very basic level. If bringing the doctors and nurses some food or dessert helped make their days better, make them *feel* better, Chan figured it would be good for Daniel. In a critical situation, he felt showing them some consideration could make all the difference.

"If the people here think about Danny a bit more, pay him a little bit of extra attention, and are a little more responsive, it's all worth it," he would tell Ken.

And so Chan started carrying in food on his visits. Lots of it. Whenever possible, he avoided standard diner-style takeout foods: burgers, fries, those sorts of things. He reasoned that nobody liked to smell other people's food, especially in stressful environments, and felt those items were "stinky."

His favorite pit stop was *Eli's Vinegar Factory*, a neighborhood gourmet shop that was close to the hospital and offered a large and appetizing selection of prepared dishes. Chan felt it would be difficult for staffers to share meals in an ICU's frenetic environment and usually purchased them in predivided, easy-to-grab portions, making sure they weren't too goopy or saucy and didn't need refrigeration. Since he never knew who would be on shift, or which other visitors would be there when he arrived, he made sure to buy different types of dishes to suit different tastes. He also bought a great many enticing desserts. They were easy for the nurses, residents, and interns to gobble on the fly and always got an enthusiastic reception.

"You'd think they would know better!" he would reflect, thinking about their happiness with the calorie-and-sugar loaded treats. "But in the end they're just people."

His strategy most assuredly wasn't hurting things for Danny; Ken and Nancy *did* notice an abundance of smiles whenever Chan appeared at the INN with his bulging grocery bags.

Chan didn't stop there. Within days of Danny's hospitalization, he had another idea. It stemmed from the awkward reluctance he had felt asking Ken for updates on Danny's condition . . . and his awareness that the Trushes were being inundated with questions about Danny from friends, acquaintances, coworkers, and their fellow parishioners at church, along with Danny's classmates and their families. Chan realized that the people around the Trushes were in a collective state of shock—and with good reason. As far as they knew, Danny had been a healthy twelve-year-old boy. And then suddenly he was . . . *what*? It was hard to grasp what was going on with him. They were desperately confused, and wanted to give their best wishes to the family, to express their caring and support. At the same time, Chan knew the Trushes were in crisis, drained, every available ounce of their energy and attention on Danny's plight. Answering all the well-intentioned questions and voice messages that had clogged their answering machine would be impossible. Chan likened the questions to someone asking a boxer how he felt in the middle of a twelve-round match. The boxer was focused on the challenge in front of him, on staying in the fight. As soon as he stopped to answer and say how he felt, a hard blow to the chin might send him reeling back on his heels. It was analogous for Ken and Nancy, who had already taken hit after hit. And they were fighting for the highest stake imaginable—their son's life.

Chan would now seek a way for everyone to express themselves in a manner that was full and enduring while being mindful of the Trushes' difficult, unpredictable situation and need for personal space. He believed that if he found the right means, people would have the generosity of spirit to put aside their own emotional needs and think first of Danny and his family.

Could the Internet be that means? Chan wondered. Could it be the *place*?

He knew that message boards on a great range of topics were sprouting up throughout cyberspace. Their formats weren't elaborate; they used default fonts such as Times Roman or Courier, and their graphics typically ranged from crude to nonexistent. People would post on a subject of interest to them, and others who shared that interest would add their messages. The boards were still largely proprietary in those days, so for the most part only subscribers to a particular service provider—America Online or CompuServe, for example—could add a message to its hosted forums. The same held for members of business or academic sites; you had to be logged in as a user before posting on one of its boards. Also, the boards were by and large just exchanges of brief messages.

A pioneer in the application of interactive technology, Chan contemplated a type of board that would have broader access than most, allowing visitors from around the Internet to read, and comment, on a lengthier post by a single author. If it worked out, Ken Trush could keep people as informed as possible about Danny on a dedicated homepage within the Agency.com site. Visitors routed from different services and networks would sign in using a password, read the update, and append their well-wishes to it. The Trushes could then check this virtual guestbook whenever they had time, taking encouragement and comfort from the warm thoughts and prayers.

Keen to see whether this latest brainstorm was feasible, Chan asked one of his web techs about it. He happily received the answer he'd wanted: "Yeah, I can do it."

It was put together quickly. Five days after Danny entered the hospital, *Daniel's Update Guestbook* was up online, which just left Chan and Ken to hash out an effective system for posting the updates. Since this was long before the widespread use of Wi-Fi technology or phone apps, Ken would not have direct access to the site at the hospital, so they decided on a combination of modern electronic communications and something like the old tried-and-true method of calling in a telegram. Chan would man the computer at his office, phone Ken, and ask what to enter. Ken would tell him, and he would read it back to make sure he'd gotten it right, then type it in.

On the afternoon of March 14, Chan clacked out the first simple post from the Trushes under the heading WISH DANIEL WELL:

Thank you for your positive thoughts. We would love it if you would ADD to this guestbook we are keeping!

Moments later in his office, Chan would do just that with another first—leaving his comment on what would be a precursor to the modern blog:

03/14/97 15:04:42 – Chan <chan@agency.com>, family friend

Dear Daniel, Michael, Nancy & Ken,

My thoughts and prayers are with you as always. I know Daniel's going to be all right. We're expecting to see Daniel running around here. We already have a spot picked out for a basketball hoop!—Chan

Ken's early posts had a deliberate similarity, an appreciative but necessarily general tone. While he was always honest, there had been little change in Daniel's condition, and he hesitated to share details that might be misinterpreted by people who were unaware of its complexities. He also realized that many visitors would be Danny's schoolmates . . . kids the same age or younger than Danny, who might be psychologically unprepared to cope with his situation or whose parents felt it would be too traumatic for them. *Danny's still asleep*, he would post, careful to avoid using the word "coma."

Ken really didn't have much else to communicate. He and Nancy had been given precious little in the way of expectations for Daniel's recovery. It was hard for them to differentiate one day from another. Their emotions seesawed. Most days the news they received wasn't good. On the better ones, they'd trust in God that everything would somehow turn out okay. On the bad ones, they would feel they couldn't go on. They were wearing down, their faith and promises being tested.

Daniel's elevated ICP had reached a critical stage. Somehow it had to be lowered if he was to have any chance of survival. As Abbott had explained on Danny's second night in the hospital— the night Ken had gone home for Nancy, thinking he was bringing her back to say good-bye to their son—when his intracranial pressure became higher than his overall blood pressure, it would interfere with, if not completely negate, his circulatory system's ability to supply his brain with blood.

As a drastic measure, the doctors decided to put him into a deeper, drug-induced coma. In essence, they were stopping all brain activity in order to combat the assault on it from within. While the drains gave the blood and fluids someplace to go, their hope was that the coma would bring the metabolic rate of his brain to a virtual standstill and reduce the swelling that had caused the pressure to rise. Danny was given an intravenous barbiturate drip of 10cc—the maximum dosage a human could withstand—and a tracheotomy to ventilate his lungs on a constant basis. In short, he was now on full life support.

For his doctors and family alike there was nothing to do but wait.

CHAPTER FIVE

And you, always wondering if we'll make it, time will tell you that I'm not giving you up, no, no, no . . .

—Gloria Estefan, "I'm Not Giving You Up"

In the silence of Danny's room, Ken quietly sang along to the music on the portable CD player. Night after night he played the same two tracks. Sometimes he'd apologize to his unconscious son for the sour notes he would hit and lament his mauling Gloria Estefan's beautiful melody. If Daniel could hear him, Ken thought, he would appreciate the lighter-side humor. He'd always been quick to laugh at something funny and fire off a comeback line.

Now Ken could only play the songs as reminders of his enduring love for his son, of his pledge to never give up hope that he'd awaken from the coma. They would calm him between his frequent prayers and his interminable hours of staring at the television set and life-support monitors, when the awareness that Danny was at death's doorstep weighed most heavily on his spirit. The only thing in his memory that had approached that barren feeling was the emptiness he'd experienced after his father's passing almost twenty years earlier, when he had also turned to music for relief, consolation, . . . and inspiration.

Nick Trush was never altogether lucid during the week he'd clung to life in the hospital after his Christmas Day heart attack. Then on the last day of December, the doctors had called to tell his mother they'd lost him. The funeral came and went, and phone calls from family and friends dwindled in frequency. Ken supposed some people were hesitant to call because they didn't really know what to say, while others just got caught up in their busy lives. Their words of support—their figurative cheering—stopped.

It was a quiet time, Ken and his mother left to grieve in solitude, his brother John having already gotten married and started a family. They didn't share their feelings of bereavement with each other; the enduring Jeanne Trush had simply wanted to move on with the rest of her life. But Ken was barely twenty-one and had never before felt such an overwhelming loss. He didn't know how to manage it, and keeping his anguish bottled up inside didn't help things.

Deep winter set in: January and February, the coldest, loneliest months of the year. Ken would toss and turn all night, sleepless and troubled, his mind returning to images of Nick in the taxi that fateful Christmas, his head flung back, his face turning blue as he gasped for air, taking what proved to be some of his last breaths. The flashbacks were vivid and constant. Laying awake in bed, his heart pierced with sorrow, Ken could almost hear his dying father ramble incoherently in the ICU.

Alone in the darkness of his room, he would listen to rock and oldies stations on the radio and sometimes play albums by favorite artists like Marvin Gaye, Diana Ross, Traffic, and The Band. The songs relaxed and soothed him. When their lyrics were particularly meaningful, they freed him from dwelling on events that couldn't be changed, and turned his thoughts toward a future that *might* yet be shaped . . . and prove happier.

Ken felt much the same way now during his bedside watches at the hospital. He didn't consciously relate Daniel's music to the songs he'd listened to in his tiny Queens bedroom back in the seventies, but he had never forgotten the power of music to heal and uplift, to soothe the soul and offer hope for a better tomorrow.

Playing it just seemed like a good thing, both for him and for Danny.

Kate Parkin, the physical therapist assigned to Daniel Trush's case, had been among the original group Fred Epstein brought over from NYU Langone. She knew Epstein and Abbott well, knew all the other doctors, nurses, and therapists, and took pride in being part of their close-knit, interdisciplinary team. In the intensive care unit, Kate and her colleagues shared a sense of mutual purpose, a cohesiveness so solid that they could practically finish each other's sentences.

Kate's acquaintance with Danny began almost from the time he entered the intensive care unit. The doctors at the INN were strong proponents of early mobilization for patients, which in plain terms meant initiating some form of physical therapy as soon as possible—often within forty-eight hours of arrival. This broad-ranging form of PT encompassed everything from easing people off breathing apparatuses to manipulating their joints to showing nurses proper ways to move their bodies and compensate for the weakness and muscle atrophy brought on by prolonged sedation or immobility. Fred Epstein and his doctors had compiled a large body of evidence substantiating that careful therapeutic interventions could improve the great majority of outcomes.

When she first saw Danny, Kate had known the twelve-year-old's prognosis was poor. He was comatose, relied on a ventilator for breathing, and had suffered horrendous bleeds in his brain. Even for someone with her training and experience, it presented a dismal picture, making his family's positive outlook all the more remarkable.

In treating the INN's young patient population, Kate had always been fueled by her own relentless optimism. She had learned from "the work," as she simply called it, that recovery from serious brain and spinal cord conditions had no clinical ceiling, even though the body's ability to repair itself had finite boundaries. It wasn't a contradictory notion. Dead brain tissue would not regenerate. Certain kinds of damage to the spine and nervous system were irreversible with known medical techniques. But Kate would have been the last person in the world to set limits on someone's capacity to regain lost *function*. Researchers hadn't altogether solved the mysteries of how the brain sent its messages through the body or seemingly compensated for the loss of neural pathways destroyed by injury or disease. Whatever progress an individual had already made in his recovery, Kate felt that if the patient and caregivers kept trying to their fullest potentials and kept challenging themselves and each other, there was room for a brighter future. For her that conviction extended beyond the hospital's sterile confines to every aspect of life; the core lesson she took from her job was that you could always improve and be a better and more productive human being.

Practically from the moment she met Daniel's parents, Kate had witnessed their readiness to learn from and assist his doctors, nurses, and therapists. Ken and Nancy were always physically, mentally, and emotionally present. They would hold Danny's hand, move his limbs, and reassure him with tender words, encouraging visitors to speak to him as well. Mindful that no one really knew how much their son could hear or understand in his comatose state, they insisted that visitors continue to interact with him, announcing themselves with a friendly "Hello Danny!" The Trushes even made sure doctors didn't say anything negative about Danny's condition within earshot of the boy.

It added up to a stimulating tactile and auditory environment, and a cooperative atmosphere that Kate would characterize as "magical"—feelings mirrored by Drs. Epstein and Abbott and the rest of the INN's staff. They saw the Trushes' supportive, goal-oriented approach as mutually beneficial, a potent recipe for success. It boosted the energy and resolve of everyone fighting to save Danny.

Kate initiated his chest physiotherapy almost at once after evaluating his case. When someone was on artificial ventilation, you wanted to strengthen his respiratory muscles, clear phlegm from his lungs, and expand them to get as much oxygen into his bloodstream and brain as possible. Kate would work on Danny for about an hour each day, rhythmically clapping on different parts of his chest, or lung fields. The accompanying manual vibration was a technique she'd been thoroughly trained to perform. With her hands flat against his chest, she would push lightly down when he exhaled, tensing and relaxing her arms to make her palms quiver. This broke apart whatever mucus might have adhered to his bronchial walls and forced it up to where it could be suctioned from his mouth.

Ken and Nancy were receptive, able students when Kate offered to teach them the two methods of chest PT. In his fragile condition, Danny couldn't afford to have congested air passages for any length of time, and they would have done anything to prevent it. But one day as Kate vibrated Danny's chest in their presence, her arms visibly trembling, a doctor came running through the door from the outer hall and shouted at her in a loud, dismayed voice.

"What are you doing? What are you doing?" He motioned at the hand she'd been pressing against Danny's chest. *"You can't have that in the ICU!"*

All three of them glanced up at him in startled confusion. Ken wondered if Kate was holding something that had escaped his notice. Then she lifted her hand off Danny to show the doctor it was empty.

He stood there in the entryway, looking slightly abashed. There were several types of mechanical oscillating devices that therapists used to loosen mucus for patients with respiratory illnesses, but they all had magnetic or electrical components that could have thrown off the readings on Danny's life-support monitors. Kate had known well enough not to bring one into intensive care, but the doctor was fooled into thinking otherwise when he'd noticed her arm shaking hard as she pressed down on her patient's chest.

Like many practicing physical therapists, Kate had very strong arms and hands.

After an awkward moment, the doctor realized his mistake and left Kate to finish her specialized massage. She would produce a wryly amused chuckle when reminded of the scene years afterward, but only until her mind turned to another vivid memory of Daniel's time in intensive care—a memory that wasn't remotely humorous to her.

It happened one morning when Kate joined Dr. Conway and a group of other ICU staffers outside Danny's room. Conway routinely convened his residents, interns, therapists, and nurses for fifteen- or twenty-minute status updates at the start of their rounds, but he seemed especially somber that day.

"You know, this kid's really, really sick," he told them in a low voice. "We need to have a conversation with the parents. Talk to them about the end of life . . . and organ donations."

Everyone looked at Conway in hushed silence. His expression left no doubt about how much it had pained him to make that declaration. But as the ICU's lead pediatric physician, he was obliged to face up to medical and statistical realities. Danny's high ICPs, and the strokes that resulted from them, had done such wholesale damage to his brain that his chances of survival were negligible.

Kate was acutely aware that the room's door was shut and that no one inside could have overheard the doctor. She also knew this was right about the time Nancy Trush would take her turn at Danny's bedside. She thought about how hard the boy's parents had been working with his medical team, how much courage they had shown, and how hopeful they'd remained in dealing with extreme, escalating adversity. The truth was that she had come to admire the kid's parents, really *admire* them, and the idea of having that talk with them wrenched at her heart. They were as resilient a couple as she'd ever met, but how did anyone bounce back from hearing their son's doctors had essentially given up on him?

Kate would never be more grateful for the INN's team spirit than at that moment. Conway was in charge of the unit. He had the final call. But on that instance he looked to his staffers for input before making his call . . . and somehow Kate and the others persuaded him to wait a bit longer.

The Trushes had been given a reprieve from hearing the worst. Kate realized it was probably a brief one. But it bought them some time, and you never knew.

Given *enough* time, she felt that improbable—and even miraculous—things could happen.

CHAPTER SIX

D r. Rick Abbott was having a long night. It was two in the morning, and Daniel's ICP was fluctuating wildly at the onset of his third week of hospitalization. For the past nine hours, Abbott and his team had labored to control the pressure without making any headway. Unless something changed soon, the rollercoaster of highs and lows would kill the boy.

Abbott had strived to get the levels in balance, get the blood circulating through Danny's brain, initiating one treatment after another to halt the deadly pattern. He'd periodically talked to the boy's mother and father to keep them abreast of his efforts but had passed on little in the way of encouragement. The positive results he'd achieved had been fleeting and inadequate.

Now, alone in his office, Abbott could not shake an overbearing sense of futility. He felt on the verge of losing the battle. The pressure in Danny's head continued to rise and fall, defying his increasingly aggressive efforts to stabilize it. He'd used all his know-how, tried every medical trick in the book. . . .

Or had he?

The memory suddenly poked at Abbott while he sat at his desk. Wasn't there something else? Something he had heard about from a colleague . . . an experimental method he'd used? With a philosophical chuckle, Abbott would later remark that it felt like divine intervention, as if a voice in his ear had whispered, "Hey, remember this? It's what you need to think about."

This was a lumbar drain, a flexible tube inserted in the small of a patient's back to allow fluid from his spine to drain out. In Daniel's case, the hope was that it would add to the room his swollen brain had at the base of his skull and consequently lower his ICP. It was a procedure Abbott's friend and fellow neurosurgeon had tried for a handful of his patients with what he'd insisted was good success.

Abbott knew that no one else in the neurological community felt it worth serious consideration, knew many who'd openly scoffed at his friend for advocating it, knew *damned well* it was frowned upon as unbelievably dangerous—and from a classic surgical perspective there was ample cause for that view. The drain's insertion was easy enough; it was hardly more than a slender catheter placed through a puncture in the skin, with a calibrated regulating tube to control the amount of spinal fluid removed. But conventional wisdom was that if you had pressure in the head and took too much fluid from the lower back, the fluid and soft tissue contents of the head would get pushed down into the spinal canal like toothpaste toward the spout of a tube. In medical school you were taught *not* to do that, since it would compress the neural structures around the brain stem, bringing about their collapse and strangulation.

Abbott acknowledged that the procedure was a desperate gamble. Still, his friend had identified certain criteria one would want to see on the patient's scans before utilizing it, a level of criticality that meant every other realistic treatment had been exhausted. Daniel's images and readings convinced Abbott he'd reached that dire juncture. He and Fred Epstein had, as Epstein would write, "never seen anyone revive from Daniel's level of cerebral damage." Their electroencephalograms, or EEGs, showed almost no electrical and brain wave activity. But if they could keep his body functioning, they could at least continue to fan a glimmer of hope.

Abbott would now spend several hours researching the procedure and flying it past his boss. Persuaded they were out of conventional options, Epstein gave his authorization, leaving Abbott only to get the Trushes onboard.

Early that morning, he emerged into the family lounge and met with both parents, Nancy having joined Ken there after dropping Mike off at school. "I'm about ready to try something that I think is crazy . . . that all my peers think is crazy, except for one guy," he told them honestly. Abbott then explained that his friend had done the procedure about seventeen or eighteen times and that, "it's worked in all but two cases." He was clear about its potential dangers, admitting the small number of patients who'd received it was a poor statistical sample that made the medical establishment's skepticism understandable.

"But that's where we're at right now," he concluded. "What do you think?"

Ken looked at him, momentarily speechless. Once again, he and Nancy faced an excruciating choice about something beyond their experience. But it was qualitatively different from when they'd okayed Dr. Berenstein's platinum coil emboliza-tion. The coiling was a proven, established technique to stop vascular bleeds. They had known that it would either succeed or fail, but probably wouldn't result in greater damage. If Abbott's plan failed, however, it might kill Danny.

What do you think?

Ken wasn't sure how to respond. It had been staggering to hear words like "collapsed brain stem." But he and Nancy didn't need long to realize they were weighing the same basic factors as before: It still came down to faith in God's will and respect for their son's medical team. That left them with another "nondecision," as Ken would put it. Abbott's commitment to saving their son was plain. And really, what else was there to do? Danny's ICP couldn't be controlled.

They signed off on the procedure at once, thinking it their only medical option.

Abbott wasted no time inserting the lumbar drain after getting their permission—and it worked perfectly. In minutes, Danny's ICP dropped to a tolerable level and remained settled throughout the day. When the familiar spike in pressure didn't recur the next night, or the next, Abbott grew encouraged the problem had been licked. It appeared the kid was going to survive. But whether he would ever come around from his coma was a different question.

Abbott and Epstein agreed it was time to begin the process of finding an answer. And that meant withdrawing Danny from the barbiturate drip.

In the days immediately after the insertion of his lumbar drain, Danny's failure to return to consciousness would blunt the Trushes' joy over his stabilized ICP. According to every electrical scan, his neural activity was almost a flat line. The cognitive exams showed no improvement in mental function. The longer he went without observable brain wave activity and awareness, the poorer the chances that he'd ever awaken. Fred Epstein—who'd gained a reputation in medical circles as a champion of lost causes—still had not entirely given up hope that Danny would recover; such an utter concession to defeat would have gone against his grain. But he acknowledged that things looked about as bad as they could.

Then, a week or so after Danny started to be weaned off the drip, it would be a weary and desperate Ken Trush who thought he saw the sign everyone had awaited—movement.

For a few seconds he just stared at his son, his heart pounding in his chest. As usual, he'd gotten precious little sleep during his nightlong watch, and he wanted to make sure his eyes weren't deceiving him. But there was no question about it. Danny's legs were moving. They bent up into a fetal position, then slid back down. Unable to suppress his euphoria, Ken hurried from the room to get the residents and nurses on shift.

With shared excitement, Ken and the medical team watched Daniel raise and lower his legs several times. But when he didn't answer after they repeatedly called his name, one of the doctors took a closer look at him, thinking she might have noticed a pattern to his movements.

As she checked Danny's vitals, Ken asked her what was happening. Looking stumped, she told him the boy's signs were fine and that she didn't think he was having a seizure of any kind. Yet he wasn't reacting to hearing his name or to her touch. In her opinion he'd shown no indications of a return to consciousness.

At last the doctor examined Danny's bladder, and the puzzlement lifted from her face. The bladder was full. When she emptied it using a bag and catheter, the movements stopped. That confirmed her suspicions. The movements were nothing more than reflex, she explained in a deflated tone. Danny's legs were rising and falling automatically. His body had been reacting to the full bladder.

Ken was crushed and didn't attempt to mask it. After the elation he had felt minutes earlier, this was a devastating comedown.

Yet it was far from the worst he'd endure over the next several days.

Almost three weeks after Danny was stricken, Drs. Epstein and Abbott reluctantly concluded they could do nothing more for him at the hospital. With his blood pressure and ICP stable, Danny might exist in a perpetual vegetative state for many years, even decades, and that would require specialized long-term care. As painful a conversation as it would be, they had a responsibility to prepare his parents "to say farewell to their elder son."

The doctors had Ken and Nancy meet with them and laid out the probable next steps. In his office, Fred Epstein explained that Danny had shown no signs of coming out of his coma. Based on all the test results, his best option for the foreseeable future would be a managed care facility.

"Children are special, you never know," he said. "But Daniel might never wake up."

Ken couldn't quite take in what Epstein had suggested. "I don't understand what you're talking about," he said. "Danny's coming home."

The doctors regarded him sympathetically. No one could be cheering for Danny louder than they were. But even if he regained full or partial consciousness, he'd almost certainly suffer from extensive motor impairment—possibly total paralysis. His parents couldn't be expected to understand the daily pressures that attending to someone in his condition would put on them. Most families shattered under the strain. In a sense, they had to be protected from their own loving instincts.

"Your son's going to require twenty-four-hour-a-day care," one of the doctors said. "The assistance of two or three people for even simple tasks like bathing. He'll have a feeding tube."

Ken hadn't been sure whether that was Epstein or Abbott. The scene in the office had taken on an otherworldliness for him. He at once was part of it, but not part of it. "We aren't writing Danny off," he insisted. "He isn't being sent to an institution."

"You don't know what you're getting into," the doctor replied. "Danny's situation could last for the rest of his life. It would be a nightmare for you and your family."

Ken and Nancy still hadn't fully absorbed the doctors' bitter outlook. They'd prayed so hard for Danny, believed in their bones that he was fighting even harder to come back to them. Wasn't signing him into a long-term facility a form of surrender? An acceptance that he'd never recover?

That was how it felt. But the Trushes trusted and respected the doctors, knew they had put their hearts and souls into saving Daniel, remembered Abbott driving in from Westchester at all hours of the night. It must have been an agonizing decision for them to call the meeting. Taking their advice seemed unfathomable . . . yet it couldn't be rejected out of hand.

"We need time to process this," Ken said, his voice dull with shock.

Epstein and Abbott expressed their understanding. The decision didn't have to be made immediately, they said.

Ken and Nancy left the office in a mental and emotional fog. Danny was their son. Their cherished creation. *A nightmare?* The most horrible one they could imagine would be losing him forever. Again, they would turn to each other for strength and support, remembering the pact they had made the day after Danny fell into a coma. And again, they would need all their faith in God to sustain them.

In Ken's secret heart, meanwhile, an unspoken prayer began to take shape. It was less than a week until Easter, a day of renewed hope and awakening possibilities, when life and faith were reaffirmed. Ken had always believed some things in life were too personal to communicate to anyone, believed sharing certain prayers with others might deprive them of their power, and he had begun appealing to God for a sign on that holiest of holy days on the Christian calendar . . . something, anything, to tell him that Daniel was still inside the unresponsive body attached to the lines and machines. That he would be able to come home to his family against every prediction.

More than at any other time since Danny's injury, Ken was praying for a miracle.

Easter Sunday fell on March 30, three weeks to the day since Daniel collapsed into his father's arms on the basketball court. After spending the night with Danny, Ken went to Mass early and prayed for the sign he'd awaited without telling anyone. Afterward, he walked straight back to Beth Israel with anticipation, even excitement, brewing at his core. He couldn't have explained his level of confidence, but he had left church truly convinced his prayers would be answered—and that the answer might be awaiting him when he returned to Danny's room. It was about ten in the morning, and he knew family and friends would arrive to visit that afternoon.

When Ken joined Nancy at Danny's bedside, his thoughts were totally on their son—but his condition was the same as it had been for the past twenty-one days. He watched Danny closely, waited, spoke to him. He might have sung to him as he so often did throughout his vigil, although he wouldn't be positive in retrospect.

For hours nothing happened. Ken's spirits gradually sunk. He began wondering if Abbott and Epstein might be right about Danny's prospects. Possibly he'd put too much focus on Easter; he felt an oppressive sense of doubt that threatened to stamp out all the hope he'd built up around the holiday.

The Trushes' visitors started coming by . . . Nancy's sister Debbie and her husband, Steve, first among them. Telling no one of his crestfallen mood, Ken rose from his seat to make room for them, just trying to be polite. Quiet, worn out, he sat at the end of Daniel's bed.

Suddenly he felt something poke his rear end. His heart jumping in his chest, he snapped his head around toward Daniel.

"Did you just kick me in my *butt*?" he blurted.

With marveling eyes, Ken saw a smile touch his son's lips. The first smile, the first genuine reaction he'd seen from him in three long weeks . . . or was it? Was it *really*? He had not forgotten the reflexive leg movements that had given him a fleeting burst of elation several nights back.

Glancing over at Nancy and his in-laws, Ken saw their astonished faces and felt his doubts subside. They'd caught the smile too.

Then—another poke.

Ken turned back to Daniel, his pulse quickening. "If you keep poking me, I'm going to have to get Grandma Jeanne to come in and talk to you," he said.

There was a second faint smile, a second gift. Grandma Jeanne was a big talker; everyone in the family knew it. And Daniel had smiled at the joke. This time it was no reflexive movement. No cruel trick of his imagination.

Ken couldn't contain himself. The boy that he and Nancy loved with all their hearts, the boy they had raised, wasn't gone. He was more than an empty shell of a person ventilated by an air pump and fed by intravenous lines. The *essential* Daniel was in there and aware of them. They had connected with him. For the next several minutes, everyone in the room tried to elicit another response from Daniel with questions, quips, anything that came to mind. But he was unresponsive. Still, Ken and Nancy were convinced of what they'd seen and could hardly wait to inform his doctors. It was the most wonderful Easter of their lives.

The next morning, near the end of his watch, Ken waited eagerly for Dr. Conway and Danny's other primary caregivers to show up at the ICU after the long holiday weekend. He was keyed up to share what had happened, to let them know Daniel was on his way back. As they filed into the ward to begin their rounds, he practically sprang from the room to tell them about Sunday's miracle.

The medical team listened, their questions measured, their faces impassive. Ken understood why they were dubious, knowing they'd seen a similar burst of excitement from him just a week before. He could only wonder how many overzealous family members they'd heard from about supposed miracles. No matter how strongly Ken insisted Danny had responded to something he had said—insisted he'd *smiled*— they had to obtain verifiable evidence.

The doctors gathered at Daniel's bedside and took turns calling his name. No answer. They checked his reflexes and got nothing more than the most basic involuntary reactions. Ken could see their doubt turning into outright skepticism . . . and concern about his emotional and psychological wellbeing. For the second time in a few days he'd seemingly over-reacted to what amounted to nothing more than muscular contractions.

It was a very strange position for Ken to find himself in: knowing what he'd observed, yet having his account met with obvious disbelief and appreciating why the doctors felt as they did.

"But what about the poke?" he said, trying his best to convince them. "The smile?" He suggested they speak to Nancy and his in-laws, insisting they'd also been witnesses.

The doctors listened calmly and quietly, then sat him down for a talk. Their guess, they said, was that his sitting down on the edge of Danny's bed had triggered a muscle spasm. Moreover, Danny's apparent smile in all likelihood bore no connection to Ken's joke about Grandma Jeanne—and wasn't really a smile. The facial movement Ken had taken for one was probably just a twitch of the lips caused by an involuntary bodily function, much the same as Danny's leg movements the week before. A filling bladder or bowels, even something like passing gas.

Ken didn't know what to say in response. Maybe the doctors were right and he'd been a victim of wishful thinking. Fatigued and confused, he didn't challenge them. But in his heart he remained convinced that what he'd seen on Sunday was real. The poke had been a poke, the smile a smile . . . the miracle a miracle.

A week later, Danny proved his father was right.

PART II

MIRACLES ON THIRTY-FOURTH STREET

CHAPTER SEVEN

On April 2, Daniel was transferred from the ICU into the intermediate, or step-down, unit next door. Still comatose, his muscles atrophied from disuse, he continued to be fed through a tube and hadn't shown any signs of coming around since the smile his family had insisted was their own Easter miracle. But his intracranial and blood pressure readings were steady, and he was breathing without mechanical assistance—qualifying him as medically stable.

Danny's new status had resulted from a judgment call by his physicians rather than a substantive change in his condition. Since he didn't require the ICU's maximal level of care, the doctors had been obliged to free a bed in the unit for another urgent admission, another kid who might show up with his life dangling by a thread. Allocation of space and resources amounted to a delicate balancing act at every busy hospital.

All that said, Daniel's relocation to the step-down unit had seemed an event worth marking to his parents. Kids in the unit did not require artificial ventilation and typically had fewer lines attached to them. And while they were under continuous observation from staffers—the large, single ward room held six to eight beds separated by curtains that were always in sight of a nurse—their bedside monitors did not have twin stations at the front desk, representing a lowered level of criticality, a reduced danger that Danny would face any sudden, life-threatening emergencies.

Ken noted Daniel's transfer in the online guestbook, while Nancy told friends that she felt his new ward should be renamed a step-*up* unit. Both of them wanted to cast Danny's progress in an encouraging light without overstating their feelings to anyone—and the truth was that, at first, there hadn't been much progress to report. The doctors had given them no real basis to believe that things were looking up, or ever would look up, for their son.

Anxious for any good word from the Trushes, their friends and relatives had been heartened by Ken's entry about the step-down move. Their comments were typically cheerful and spangled with exclamation points. One post from an adult read:

Hey, Daniel, I was so psyched to hear you are out of intensive care! That's excellent! It sounds like you're off to a great start!

Danny's classmates were also buoyant, but they mostly stuck to the standard topics of preadolescent concern—sports and classes:

Hi, Dan. I see that you are doing better every day. The Knicks are playing Orlando tonight and are two games behind Miami. The Yanks are 1-1, they lost their first game to Seattle 4-2, but then they came back in the next game and clobbered them 16-2. The Mets are 0-2 but still my favorite team. Gotta go to Math now (let me tell you, you are lucky for missing that). See ya!

When Daniel's eyes opened after a few days in the step-down unit, and then opened again soon afterward—each time for a few short minutes—his medical team urged Ken and Nancy to keep their emotions in check. Their cognitive tests showed the boy to be in a perpetual vegetative state, in which open-eyed intervals were termed a condition of "wakeful unawareness" that was barely different from a coma. His gaze wasn't tracking objects or people. He had a blank, glassy stare and no expression on his face. Given the wholesale damage to Danny's brain, his doctors felt the odds were heavily stacked against his recovering more than a low level of mental and physical function.

This did not mean Dr. Epstein had entirely dismissed what Ken, Nancy, and their visitors had claimed to witness on Easter. If they'd in fact seen Daniel smile, and it has been a real smile and not a reflexive twitch of his lips, then it gave Epstein a bit of guarded optimism. A sense of humor required a complex cognitive architecture, an ability to pick up on the different associations that made a joke funny. *Did you just kick my butt?* For Danny to have been amused by his worried father's remark while he lay helpless in his sickbed, all the mental processes associated with a sense of humor necessarily had to be intact. That led Epstein to believe that the fundamental person he'd been before March 9 could have survived the multiple strokes, could have made it *through* . . . all assuming that the boy's family hadn't imagined the smile. Epstein could only wait and see.

A week passed without a noticeable change. Daniel was moved again, this time from the step-down unit to a private room up the hall. As when he'd left the ICU, the transition was entirely based on Daniel's medical stability. His doctors had no evidence that he was emerging from his vegetative state and offered little to encourage his parents he ever would.

Daniel's lack of improvement put Ken and Nancy under mounting pressure. He was almost ready to be discharged, leaving them to weigh the feasibility of bringing him home against the prospect of having him admitted to a long-term care facility. To compound things, they knew their health insurer's coverage of his hospital stay was constantly being monitored and reviewed, and that it might soon reach its limit. While their case manager had shown understanding and compassion in approving his medical treatments, the doctors at Beth Israel had now done all they could for Daniel. Whatever lay ahead was in the hands of God, his family, his therapists, and his own inner strength. This undeclared deadline challenged the Trushes' resolve and at times threatened to make the bright promise of Easter Sunday seem like a shrinking light in their rearview mirror.

Meanwhile, they took their turns watching over Daniel with friends and relatives often stopping by the hospital during the day. Since the private rooms didn't have convertible chairs like the ICU and step-down unit, Ken slept on a mattress that he'd brought in from up the hall and laid on the floor near Daniel's bed. It was a taxing, scary period for him. With Daniel no longer connected to life-support monitors, and his nursing observation downscaled to a single nurse on two-hour rounds, Ken became his de facto night care. While he would occasionally drift off into a flimsy, restless sleep, a part of him remained constantly alert to everything that was going on in the room. It was as if he'd developed a sixth sense.

One night while Ken was dozing, that near-extrasensory awareness saved his son's life. Danny was in trouble. Without knowing how or why or even consciously realizing he'd picked up on his distress signals, he jolted awake and sprang over to the bed.

Daniel had vomited in his sleep and was choking on saliva and stomach acids. Acting at once, Ken turned the boy's head sideways, recalling Teddy Frischling's instructions the day Danny collapsed in the gym. Then he pushed the bedside emergency button.

The nurses quickly arrived and suctioned out Danny's airway. In moments he was back to resting comfortably.

Ken returned to his mattress on the floor, newly reminded of his son's fragility. What would have happened if he hadn't been in the room? Or if he'd been sound asleep?

The unspeakable scenarios played in Ken's mind for hours as he lay staring up at the paneled ceiling, watching daylight spread thinly across it from the windows.

The days and nights wore on. Danny's eyelids now began opening more regularly for brief intervals. It often occurred between 9:30 and 10:30 p.m. when the hospital was quiet— and *most* often when Ken was speaking to him alone and trying to gently elicit responses. His gaze remained vague, but Ken was convinced he'd been seeing small facial movements in reaction to things he said, subtle hints that Danny was aware of his presence. In his heart, he felt his son was trying to let him know he heard him and just needed time to regain the strength to communicate. But when the doctors arrived early in the morning, he was invariably fast asleep.

Then one day they came in while Danny's eyes were still open. Ken couldn't control his excitement. For the first time since the episode in the step-down unit, they had found him awake. Ken had gotten used to having his reports met with doubt but felt the doctors seeing Danny's facial expressions might persuade them he was making a comeback.

"What color is your dad's shirt?" one of them began.

Danny stared vacantly, his features unmoving.

"Danny, is it light or dark outside?" the doctor asked.

No reply.

The doctor tried urging more answers from Danny without success. She moved her finger across Danny's eyes, shone a light into them to see how his pupils reacted. Ken noticed that Danny was perspiring and mentioned it to the doctors, but they didn't seem to think it significant. After a few minutes they asked to speak with him out in the hall.

"Daniel isn't consciously registering our questions," said the one who'd examined him. "Ken, I'm sorry, but it's also likely he's lost his eyesight." The doctor explained that she'd based her opinion on Danny's reactions and on the brain scans showing severe damage to his optical centers.

Ken listened in silence. Danny had already weathered many life-threatening crises. He and Nancy felt blessed he was alive. They believed Danny was waking up, and nothing anyone said would dissuade them from that belief.

He refused to jump to conclusions. If the essential Danny was still whole—and Ken was positive he *was*—then why might his vision not be intact as well?

But Ken had something else to consider. Daniel's discharge, and with it the hardest decision of his parents' lives, loomed ahead as an unavoidable and intimidating crossroad. In that all-important respect, his failure to respond to the doctor's questions had been a disappointment.

Ken and Nancy believed Danny was still there. But for all their insistence and tenacity, they knew time was running out for him to convince the INN's medical team.

———————

It was mid-April, over a month after Daniel had been sped to Beth Israel in an ambulance. His condition seemed unchanged since he'd left the step-down unit, with his doctors concurring that his open-eye periods weren't necessarily associated with a return of cognitive function and that he was probably sightless. Instead, they felt that the near-clockwork regularity of those periods, which still mostly occurred at night, probably arose from a primitive mechanism in the brain stem that controlled his sleep-wake cycles. Called the reticular activating system, its neural circuits caused the eyelids to open and shut at intervals and just gave Daniel the appearance of true wakefulness. Without medical indications to the contrary, the doctors could reach no other conclusion.

The Trushes understood their reasoning. At the same time, they were undaunted in their belief that Danny was working his way back. The hardest thing about the disparity between their observations and what the doctors considered evidence was that it sometimes made them feel that what they saw from Daniel was being dismissed as wishful thinking.

One Sunday, when Ken and his brother-in-law Steve were in the hospital room, a Knicks game on the television set, Ken was using a sponge applicator to wet Daniel's lips and tongue. For weeks Daniel had gotten all his nourishment through a tube. Until the doctors learned whether he could physically swallow, they had insisted he couldn't have anything in his mouth. Ken and Nancy were even under strict instructions to refrain from brushing his teeth as a precaution against him choking on toothpaste or his own saliva. They could only swab out Daniel's mouth with a green foam pad on an applicator stick, doing it often each day as they took their turns at his side.

Ken was typically methodical using the applicator. He dipped the sponge in a cup of water, touched its green foam pad to his son's lips, and then slowly moved it in a circle around his mouth.

Whether awake or asleep, Danny would usually part his lips once they were wet. Then Ken would press the sponge against his tongue and moisten it. When he did that, Daniel sometimes clamped down on the pad with his back teeth as if to thirstily squeeze out every last drop of water. He'd done it repeatedly that day, his eyes devoid of expression.

Ken swabbed his mouth several times while talking to Steve during the game. On the fifth or sixth go 'round, he was bringing the moistened sponge toward Danny's lips when the boy's mouth suddenly opened.

Ken and Steve broke off their conversation in midsentence, looking at each other with incredulity. Just days earlier, Ken had been told that Daniel was likely blind. But he had opened his mouth an instant *before* Ken touched the applicator to it. They didn't need a detective to tell them he'd seen the moistened sponge in his father's hand, *seen* it coming toward his mouth, and readily accepted it. *Seen.* In their minds, what else could it mean?

Ken got up and ran into the hall to find a staff doctor. But, as had often happened, Daniel didn't repeat what he'd done for the resident. After shining a penlight in his eyes and moving it from side to side, the doctor gave Ken the sort of dubious look that had become all too familiar to him and his family. Daniel hadn't tracked the beam. Unable to confirm what Ken and Steve told him, the doctor wasn't convinced the boy could see.

Although disappointed, the Trushes remained positive. In eight days, Daniel would be thirteen years old, and they intended to create a cheerful, stimulating environment in his hospital room and celebrate the occasion with close relatives, friends, gifts, colorful balloons, and a birthday cake.

Danny was already surrounded by plenty of letters and get-well cards. Ken and Nancy had been prohibited from bringing too many items into the imposed sterility of the ICU and step-down unit, but with the rules relaxed in Daniel's private room, they'd been papering the walls with them. Danny had received dozens and dozens of cards from friends, family members, and people around the world he'd never met who had shared their prayers for him through word of mouth and Internet communications. At the Trushes' parish church, Our Lady of Good Counsel, Father Keane would recite a special prayer for Daniel at his daily Mass. Ken and Nancy considered this collective outpouring of kindness a tangible force for their son's recovery that came bundled in love and the abiding hope for a miracle.

And then there were the names on the walls. Ken and Nancy had started noticing them soon after Daniel's transfer. Written in different handwritings, some printed, others in script, the signatures were marked in ink on the wall near the room's entrance. When the Trushes asked Danny's nurses and aides about them, they were told they'd been left by young patients who had previously occupied the room and signed their names on discharge. The signing was a traditional rite of passage at the INN, an assertion of courage and will and battles well fought by children too young to have any business fighting them. As the days passed, Ken and Nancy would hear their stories from the staff and want to find out more about what happened to each child after leaving the hospital. They were sometimes saddened but always inspired.

That inspiration took a giant step toward fulfillment on the night of Tuesday, April 13, one that at first mirrored many of those that preceded it. Ken had spent several hours talking to Daniel from his bedside. Then sometime after ten o'clock, Daniel opened his eyes and began silently moving his lips. Ken watched him carefully, struggling to keep his expectations in check. This had happened before without Daniel really coming around.

Danny's mouth worked, opening and closing. He had a surgical hole, or stoma, in the middle of his throat from the tracheotomy, as well as a short tube that obstructed his vocal cords. His lips, gums, tongue, and throat were still slightly swollen and parched after weeks of taking in fluids exclusively through an IV line. Even if he was regaining consciousness, it would have been hard for him to make a sound.

Hard, yes. But was he *trying*?

Ken waited. When Danny answered his unvoiced question, mouthing his first words in over a month, his voice was a dry, barely audible whisper.

"I can't talk," he said.

Ken looked down at him, his emotions going a series of rapid swings; disbelief turned into joy, then plunged off into heart-rending sadness as his eyes went to Danny's eyes. They were looking up at his face, seeing it, confirming what Ken had already believed—Danny still had his sight. But the frustration in his gaze was immeasurable.

I can't talk.

The first time the doctor had checked Danny's eyes, Ken had noticed the perspiration dripping down his face. He'd been sure his son had been sweating with exertion, summoning every ounce of his inner strength in an effort to communicate. But what would he be thinking right now? He'd fought his way to the surface only to find himself without a voice. There was no way he could possibly know about the tracheotomy. He'd been comatose when the procedure was performed.

Ken gathered his wits, searching for the right words to calm him. "You have a trach hole in your throat," he explained finally.

"The doctors put it there to help you breathe, but they can close it. The air's coming out before it gets to your mouth. That's why you can't talk."

A moment passed. Danny didn't try to speak again, and his eyes were still fixed and staring. But Ken thought he saw understanding replace his confusion.

"In the morning you'll have to show the doctors that you can speak," he went on. "They think I'm a loony tune."

His son visibly settled . . . and then he grinned. A broad, contagious grin of amusement that was all Daniel. It spread from his face to Ken's. And then Ken was laughing aloud, and Danny's grin grew wider, and that made Ken laugh even harder.

After the repeated, massive assaults on his brain and body—the hemorrhages, strokes, and drugs—Daniel had broken through with three words that, for Ken, might as well have been the Gettysburg Address. Smiling, laughing together in shared relief, both father and son knew it was a moment they would cherish as long as they lived.

––––––––––

Long before Danny's primary doctors began to show up at the hospital the next morning, Ken had excitedly called Nancy with the news that their son was back. But even amid this elation, he realized the doctors still had to be convinced.

Ken told them what happened the previous night, fearing he would meet with their skepticism—the tired-out boy was fast asleep, showing no outward sign that he'd spoken just hours before. But while the doctors may have been cautious, they were ready to perform a simple test. If Danny was in fact trying to speak, they said, plugging his trach tube would make things a lot easier for him. First, however, a respiratory specialist had to ascertain that Danny's upper airway was clear. Also, Epstein and Abbott needed to give their okays. Even if all went well, Ken was told it might be hours before anything was done.

At noon Nancy arrived from The Brick School to take over the watch from Ken, who headed off to work. She would keep him updated throughout the day as the doctors examined Danny and conferred with one another about the procedure. In the early afternoon, they decided to move forward.

By now Danny was awake—until that point, a rarity during the day—but he'd been staring without much expression and hadn't spoken at all. The doctors explained what they were about to do, uncertain whether he could understand them but following Ken and Nancy's groundwork of always engaging him as if he could. The capping trial was a quick enough procedure; with Abbott present, a small plastic plug was pushed into the hole in Danny's throat to externally close off the trach tube. If Danny started coughing or labored for breath, the plug would be taken off and the trach tube reopened. If he had no problems, the tube would be removed from his throat after a week or two's evaluation.

The plug inserted, Daniel drifted off to sleep, breathing easily. Nancy settled into her vigil. There was nothing to do but wait. In the past few weeks, she and Ken had turned waiting into an art form.

It was a while before Danny woke up. But soon after his eyelids finally snapped open, he spoke again. Hoarse, ragged at the edges, his voice was stronger than the night before. This time he put all his effort into getting out a single word:

"Mommy."

Nancy's eyes blurred over. "I'm here," she said.

The tears were streaming down her face when she called Ken's office a few minutes later.

CHAPTER EIGHT

I n the third week of April, visitors to Daniel's online guest-book were thrilled and delighted by the announcement that he'd finally spoken. The Trushes had reported little after his transfer from the ICU, and with the frequency of Ken's posts having dwindled, many had worried that his son's improvement had stalled—or worse, advanced as far as it ever would. Now the sudden good news brought renewed congratulations and encouragements (*"Mommy" is a really good word to say after all you've been through. It's terrific that you said something. Soon you'll be talking at full strength and energy.*), along with a fresh round of sports updates from Danny's school buddies. (*Tiger Woods won the Masters in golf. The Knicks have been playing really well. The Yankees are okay. Andy Pettitte is the first player to be 3-0.*)

With word of Daniel's breakthrough circulating among his family and friends, Ken and Nancy readily welcomed company to his hospital room. But he was often asleep and didn't say much when he was awake. Unable to voluntarily move his arms and legs, or even turn his head, Daniel mostly stared as in previous days. In their eagerness to prove he was on his way back, his parents were occasionally disappointed when he didn't speak to his visitors. In that regard they were average members of the TV generation that, reared on movies of the week, expected reviving coma patients to wake up and talk all in a few minutes' time. But as their son's recovery progressed, they gradually brought their expectations in line with reality. It was unfair to wish for Danny to perform like an actor following a director's cues. Whether from boredom, fatigue, or his occasionally being in no *mood* to talk, he wasn't always communicative, and they just had to accept it. Ken was also fairly certain the capped tracheotomy tube in place above his larynx made speaking uncomfortable and difficult for him.

Daniel needed to regain his stamina, needed to mend. At the same time, Ken wanted to gauge his son's present capabilities and urge him forward. To challenge him to keep getting better. It was the way he'd always approached things: mapping out the path ahead, setting goals, and embracing the challenge of achieving them. He believed that goals not only couldn't be rigid but shouldn't be. Everything in life, every person, had limitations. But Ken was convinced that people's limits, like their goals, could always change and evolve. Danny had suffered extensive brain damage. The scans didn't lie. But what were his limits . . . and more importantly, what was his *potential?*

One night when he had been up for awhile, Ken decided to give him a basic math quiz.

"What's two plus two, Daniel?" he asked. "You can blink your answers. One blink for the number one, two blinks for two, and so on."

Daniel responded immediately and blinked four times. The right answer.

His father smiled. "Great," he said. "Now how much is two plus one?"

Daniel blinked three times.

"How about three plus two?"

Five blinks.

Ken felt a surge of excitement. He remembered his prayers alongside Daniel's bed when he'd been comatose, the long wait for any sign that he might be awakening, and was filled with appreciation and gratitude for the gift he'd just received. It was a feeling Nancy shared when he gave her the news.

As Danny's wakeful stretches grew longer over the next several nights, Ken tested him with more simple additions. He answered them all correctly. It was the same when Ken tried subtraction exercises. He got every answer right and seemed to enjoy it.

Encouraged, Ken decided to see whether Daniel might use eyeblinks to respond to nonarithmetical questions. He stuck to basics again: One blink meant *yes,* and two meant *no.*

"Are you feeling okay, Dan?"

He responded with a single blink.

"Do you have any headaches?"

Two blinks.

"Anything bothering you?"

Two blinks.

Pleased, Ken changed the subject. "That's great," he said. "Were you happy to see Mike today?"

One blink.

"How about when Uncle Steve and Uncle John were here? Weren't they really funny?"

One blink . . . and then a faint smile.

Ken's heart soared. Even while Daniel had lain in a deep coma, the two men had lightened the mood in his room with a mock rivalry, hoping their banter would get through to him. Their running competition always started with one or the other asking Danny which of them was his favorite uncle. Then either John or Steve would rattle off a list of reasons why *he* deserved the title, milking the comical routine for all it was worth.

For Ken, Daniel's response was doubly gratifying. Besides having elicited an appropriate response, he'd managed to bring a smile to his son's face. It gladdened him to no end.

Unfortunately Danny's success with eyeblink communication was more erratic during the day. With his doctors in the room, he would sometimes respond to questions with the right number of blinks, sometimes not. On a few instances he started blinking uncontrollably. While that left the doctors questioning his engagement in Ken's math problems, his parents weren't discouraged. They realized they were pushing him and that he was pushing himself even harder. Every blink of his eyes represented an act of will. Every command his brain sent through his weakened, skeletal body meant firing up neural pathways and muscle groups that had been dormant for weeks, or possibly opening new paths to replace his damaged ones. It was natural that there would be misfires.

By now Ken and Nancy had realized their son's journey would defy predictable directions or imposed timetables. Eventually the rest of world would see it too. They didn't know where that journey was leading their family or what unknown hurdles they might face through its twists and turns. But each step, each *accomplishment*, was something magical to celebrate. They were convinced that with faith and unconditional love for Danny, things would work out okay.

Meanwhile, it hadn't escaped them that the latest, very large step in Daniel's journey had occurred right in time for his thirteenth birthday, a milestone that was also in the thoughts of one of his most beloved relatives: Nancy's octogenarian father, Joseph Pepe Hosnedl, a.k.a. Grandpa Pepe.

———————————

Grandpa Pepe was thinking Daniel could use a Tic Tac. He knew that rules were rules at the INN. But one morning in Danny's room, his eyes fell on the youngster's dry, chapped lips, and he got an idea that bending the rules ever so slightly wouldn't be such a crime.

With his wife Eva, and daughter Diane, Grandpa Pepe had become a fixture at Danny's bedside. Short, gray haired, and quick to smile, Pepe had raised his family working a series of blue-collar jobs in the same Manhattan neighborhood where his grandson was hospitalized. Pepe loved to whistle and sing the old standards, just as he'd once done while selling Christmas trees out on the wintry street. Otherwise he was a reserved, quiet man . . . although two reliable ways to bring out his vocal side were to mention his beloved New York Yankees or coax him into playing a game of blackjack.

Now Eva and Diane were off somewhere running errands, and Ken and Nancy had stepped out of the room, leaving Pepe alone with an awake but quiet Daniel. The boy's mouth was so dried out . . . Pepe had noticed there wasn't a drop of moisture in it. The sight had made his heart ache.

Grandpa Pepe knew the rules. No solids, no liquids, no brushing his teeth, nothing. Still, the youngster's thirteenth birthday was just days away on April 21. It was a big occasion, entering his teens, and he deserved a treat. The tiny mint would dissolve before he could swallow it anyway. What was the harm in giving him one?

Pepe made his decision. Reaching into his pocket for the container, he thumbed open its lid, shook a Tic Tac into his hand, and carefully slipped it into Danny's lips with his fingertips.

Ken and Nancy walked through the door just as Danny started moving his mouth around the candy. They hurried to the bed, looked down at their son, looked up at Pepe. Their expressions left no doubt they were upset.

"What's that in Daniel's *mouth*?" Nancy demanded

Grandpa Pepe stood there facing both parents. They appeared on the verge of panic.

"Ahh . . . his mouth looked dry, so I gave him a Tic Tac," he explained awkwardly. What else could he tell them? The mint had *seemed* like a good idea. To him, anyway. "I think he likes it."

Ken and Nancy had shifted their eyes back to Daniel, wondering whether to hit the emergency button to call for a nurse. But a moment later they both exhaled. Their son wasn't gagging or having any other difficulties. The mint had started to harmlessly dissolve in his mouth.

Nancy turned back to her father, saw the hapless look on his face . . . and suddenly burst out laughing. A moment later, Ken started in too. They were cracking up. And Pepe's unchanging expression only made them laugh harder.

"*I think he likes it*," Nancy said when she caught her breath, mimicking his defensive tone. "*I think he LIKES it!*"

Then she and Ken were laughing together again, their tension dissipating into the air. After so many long, anxious days and nights, it came as a welcome relief—a kind of exhalation. They would repeat Pepe's words for a long time afterward, always with his inflections and mannerisms, and get a kick out of it every time.

Soon afterward, in fact, they would even take some inspiration from him . . . and wind up in some hot water of their own.

———————

Their surprise at catching Grandpa Pepe red-handed aside, Ken and Nancy had realized he'd acted wholly out of kindness. He'd felt for the boy and wanted to help him. Besides, they thought, Daniel *had* seemed to like the mint.

Soon they began wondering if Pepe might not have been too far off the mark. After weeks without solid food, Daniel still hadn't had anything in his mouth but foam swabs. They'd tried hard to stimulate all his senses from Day One of his hospital stay, but it occurred to them that his sense of taste had been neglected. Necessarily, yes, and under doctor's orders. Yet neglected even so. Say they gave him a lollipop instead of a piece of loose candy? Something he couldn't swallow? Practically speaking, it seemed as safe as using a tasteless swab. They could put it in Danny's mouth so he could work up some moisture and enjoy its sugary sweetness, then take it out whenever they wanted. As long as they were careful to hold onto the stick, it made perfect sense.

Within a few days of the Great Tic Tac Incident, Ken and Nancy—along with Nancy's sister Debbie—brought, not to say smuggled, a cherry lollipop into the hospital. Though Daniel was quiet throughout the morning, he was awake with his eyes open, as he'd been when his grandfather was there to visit.

Nancy slipped the pop into his mouth, thinking she'd let it rest there and melt away on his tongue. And at first things went even better than expected.

"Look." Nancy said. She smiled with delight. "He's licking it!"

Debbie and Ken huddled closer to Daniel's bedside. Now they were smiling too. His tongue moved lightly over the lollipop. Their idea had worked like a charm!

They were still beaming over their success when Danny suddenly clamped the pop between his teeth.

Nancy tried to pull the lollipop from his mouth. It didn't budge. Danny lay there with the white lollipop stick poking straight up of lips,

"Ken!" she blurted, still tugging on the stick. "Daniel won't let go of the pop!"

Ken took hold of the stick and pulled. The lollipop stayed put, Danny's molars chomping down on the pop's cherry-colored head.

Growing anxious, Ken massaged Danny's jaw to relax it. When that didn't work, he tried prying it open, as the boy's orthodontist had done while removing his braces. But Danny didn't open his mouth.

Ken exchanged mortified glances with Nancy and his sister-in-law. Daniel wasn't gagging on the lollipop and wouldn't as long as they held onto the stick so he didn't swallow it. But what if the doctors or nurses came in? What would they think?

"I'll tickle him," Debbie said. She'd gotten reactions out of Danny before by tickling his toes. Why not give it a try?

She scooted around to the foot of the bed and tickled Danny. Nothing. His jaws stayed locked, the pop firmly wedged between his molars.

Ken was stumped. Pulling, prying, massaging, and tickling hadn't worked. *What now?*

Across the bed, Nancy saw his face screw up with frustration and abruptly started laughing despite her frenzied state of mind ... laughing even harder than she had at her father. After all the ribbing Pepe had taken from them, they'd broken the rules themselves and managed to trump his crazy idea with a crazier one of their own.

Now Ken was also laughing, and a second later Debbie joined him. The three of them couldn't collect themselves. Their predicament was beyond ridiculous. It wouldn't be long before somebody from the hospital's staff showed up and saw them scrambling around the bed. Worse, Ken had suddenly realized the doctors would know what they'd done even if they did manage to get the pop out . . . the bright *cherry red* pop Daniel had been licking before he chomped down on it. His matching red tongue would be a dead giveaway. Why hadn't that occurred to any of them?

They went back to trying to wrestle the pop from Danny's mouth . . . and then, almost to their astonishment, he released it. Just opened his mouth wide enough for Ken to quickly to pull it out.

He looked at Nancy and her sister again. The bright red, partially dissolved, slightly goopy pop in his hand might as well have been a World Series championship trophy. Neither Ken nor Nancy nor Debbie had the slightest clue what had gotten Danny to give it up. They couldn't even have said his jaw grip on the pop had been voluntary.

But voluntary or involuntary . . . boy, oh boy, had he *ever* seemed to enjoy it.

Daniel's thirteenth birthday celebration was a free-flowing affair, with a cake, helium balloons, and loads of gifts—including an extensive wardrobe of Knicks, football Giants and Yankees regalia. People came and went throughout the day in keeping with the INN's open visitor policy and the Trushes' welcoming attitude. Ken and Nancy didn't know who would show up, when their company would get there, or how long anyone would stay. It set the celebration apart from traditional birthday parties, when people showed up at a designated time, sang Happy Birthday, blew out candles, and watched the guest of honor open his presents. Ken thought the loose, unpredictable feel was exhilarating, exhausting, and fun.

Danny himself was only alert for portions of the day. But he was surrounded by true, heartfelt expressions of love, and that made it a joyous occasion for the Trushes—and an appropriately memorable one to mark the arrival of his teen years.

Happy Birthday, Daniel. Your progress inspires us all, wrote one of the many friends and relatives to post on his online board.

That perfectly summarized the feelings of everyone who knew him.

———————

As April came to an end, Drs. Epstein and Abbott had once again started to discuss the next step in Daniel's treatment with his parents. They now agreed there was evidence he had some awareness of himself and his environment. That was more than anyone on their team had expected when the boy's brain was being savaged nightly by a soaring ICP and massive strokes and his doctors were unable to detect any signs of consciousness. Back then it had seemed improbable that Danny would preserve even a minimal level of cognitive function. His progress so far gave the doctors hope that he could continue to improve.

They were less clear about predicting the outer boundaries of Daniel's improvement—in other words, how far he might go toward enjoying a high quality of life. His four remaining aneurysms were potential time bombs in his head, and it was Epstein's recommendation that they be clipped off when he was strong enough. But that was at least four or five months in the future and would be predicated on Daniel making steady gains. In his present state the eight-hour surgery was out of the question.

The doctors were also cautious when advising Ken and Nancy about the best place for his rehab therapy. Epstein's background at NYU Langone Medical Center had given him longstanding ties to its Rusk Institute of Rehabilitation Medicine's pediatric unit, one of the top ten centers in the country for the treatment of children with disabilities. But Epstein and his medical staff didn't believe Danny could tolerate Rusk's highly intense course of physical therapy and instead suggested that the Trushes look into Blythedale Children's Hospital in Westchester, New York. The state's only facility dedicated exclusively to children with "complex rehabilitative needs," Blythedale had a solid reputation.

A drive out to the hospital left Ken and Nancy unenthusiastic. It was nearly thirty miles outside the city. They couldn't reconcile themselves to leaving Daniel there alone, so far away from home. And how would his family be able to regularly visit him?

The Trushes came away feeling better after they investigated their second option, Saint Mary's Hospital for Children. The hospital specialized in pediatric traumatic brain injury and coma recovery. It had an impressive staff and was closer to home, in the borough of Queens. But was it close enough? When Ken was at work, Nancy, Diane and their elderly parents would have to take a train and bus out to see Daniel. It would be a long trek for his school friends, who were currently within walking distance of the hospital, and whose parents would have to carve out significant chunks of time to bring them on visits. In their deep-seated belief that love, caring, and socialization were keys to their son's healing, Ken and Nancy once again worried that he'd be deprived of those keys.

While they struggled with the dilemma of where to place Danny, Ken went on sleeping in his room every night, and his physicians initiated a final round of evaluations to confirm his readiness for discharge—and to use as gauges of his overall health and rehab potential. Among the most critical was a video fluoroscopic swallowing exam (VFSE).

The ability to swallow is frequently impaired in traumatic brain injury victims. The loss can be permanent or temporary, whole or partial. With the VFSE, a small morsel of food coated with a metallic substance called barium sulfate is lowered down the throat to trigger the swallowing reflex. Opaque to x-rays, the barium will leave traces in the patient's pharynx and esophagus when he swallows, giving radiologists a clear, real-time visualization of the food's movement. It will also show if any food is being aspirated—drawn into the airways, or trachea and lungs, instead of the patient's gastrointestinal tract.

Ken and Nancy were allowed to observe the procedure from beginning to end. It was staggering to see their son's jaw open up onscreen, and then watch the involuntary contractions in his throat and esophagus transport the food down to his stomach. Until that time, Ken's only mental reference for that sort of imagery had been Halloween costumes, horror films, and perhaps a skeleton in biology class. Seeing his son's head and upper body like that made his mouth drop. The image wasn't recognizable as Danny. He could have been anybody.

For Ken, it was a startling reminder that people all looked pretty much the same stripped down to muscles, bone, tendons, and cartilage. Daniel—the real Daniel—wasn't the fragile biological assembly revealed by the x-rays. What made him who he was, what Ken saw as the things that define every human being, were the mind and spirit within that fragile structure. And it was his son's strength of spirit, his enduring life force that had carried him on through the worst.

The test results were positive. Daniel had normal swallowing functions. But the experience left his parents so overwhelmed it would be a while before the good news sank into their minds.

On April 25—the last Friday of the month—Nancy and Ken decided to ask Michael if he wanted to sleep over at the hospital. Mike's young life had dramatically changed, and while he'd adapted in a remarkably accepting, unselfish way, his parents thought the sleepover would be nice, giving him a measure of restored normalcy—if only for a single night. It seemed an eternity since he'd sat watching TV on the sofa with his dad and big brother.

Mike jumped at the suggestion. Since the day of Dr. Conway's anatomy lesson, he'd been at Beth Israel every afternoon, keeping Daniel company and trying to lift everyone's spirits. As Daniel had improved and many of his classmates had started coming by to visit, Mike gained a receptive audience for his efforts. When he noticed his brother's hair was growing out, Mike joked that he was going to invite eager "Republican barbers" to remedy it with their scissors. Then maybe somebody like Senator Bob Dole, who'd been a football end in college (and had a notoriously bad Republican haircut) might offer to take Daniel to a football game.

With his drifting in and out of consciousness, Danny hadn't always responded to the wisecracks. But after Mike saw him smile at one after his birthday, he picked up their pace.

It always made him sad to leave Daniel behind when he went home, though. And he hardly ever saw his dad, who'd spent every night at the hospital for nearly two months. Staying with them would be a special treat.

Late Friday afternoon, after Danny's other visitors left, Mike had dinner at the hospital with his father. Then he excitedly settled in for "Guys' Night."

Ken made things feel as normal as possible. He picked up a VHS recording of the Tom Cruise action film *Mission Impossible*, rolled a larger television and videocassette player into the room, and they watched the movie from beginning to end, Ken and Mike scarfing down their favorite junk foods. Danny only had his eyes open part of the time, but the important thing for Mike and his father—and Daniel too, they felt—was that they were all together, just like in the old days before Danny's injury.

When the movie was over, Mike tucked in beside his father on the floor and had his soundest sleep in weeks. Saturday morning, Ken walked him over to a local diner, where they ordered a takeout breakfast of omelets and vanilla milkshakes for three and then brought it back to the hospital room. Daniel, who'd been cleared to eat solid foods after he passed the swallowing test, didn't seem too interested in the omelet, but the shake was another story altogether; he got a fair amount of it down through his straw.

The sleepover was another little thing that meant so much to Ken—a special night with both his sons, and the first time since Danny's injury that felt like *old* times.

Almost.

———————

With Daniel's positive VFSE results and encouraging progress toward a higher level of function, Drs. Epstein and Abbott guardedly reassessed their opinion that he'd be unable to tolerate the Rusk Institute's demanding therapeutic regimen. They still felt it was a long shot given his frail physical condition and varying states of alertness. But Ken and Nancy's lukewarm reaction to Blythedale and St. Mary's, and a consultation with Danny's ICU therapist, Kate Parkin, and Chief Physiatrist Lori Garjian persuaded the doctors there was no downside to giving Danny a referral. It would be left to the center's intake people to determine whether their program was a viable choice for his rehab.

After a review of Daniel's medical records, Rusk informed his doctors that they would consider his application. The next step would be a face-to-face meeting with his parents. Rusk was a six-story building on 34th Street overlooking the East River Drive, part of the NYU Langone Medical Center in midtown Manhattan. In a visit to its thirty-five bed pediatric therapy, or Ped, wing, housed on the fifth floor, Ken and Nancy were given a tour of the facility before sitting down with its social workers to discuss their son's eligibility.

The caseworkers were frank about their reservations. Their institute's rigorous, goal-oriented program would require Daniel to participate in therapy for a minimum of three hours a day, with an added two to three hours of optional therapies. The interdisciplinary plan—tailored to each child—would be a mix of physical therapy, occupational therapy, speech therapy, psychotherapy, and other specialized rehabilitative treatments. Like his doctors, the intake people at Rusk questioned whether all that would be too much for Daniel. His hospital records described a child whose ability to function had been severely compromised. He was physically frail, bedridden, and barely responsive to environmental stimuli and personal communication. If accepted for their program, Daniel would start his treatment at ground zero and need to overcome a plethora of obstacles as he advanced.

Offsetting these concerns—to a degree—were Daniel's confirmed strengths. His health and developmental histories prior to his injury were normal for a boy his age. His Dalton report cards described a quick learner with a humorous, spirited nature and an enthusiastic attitude toward his studies. Daniel's recommendation from Beth Israel had stressed that his family had been loving and supportive throughout his stay and that his friends and classmates had matched their support. Motivation was at the heart of Rusk's approach, and the caseworkers could see that he'd been a smart, focused, hardworking kid with a lot of initiative.

They could also plainly see how much Ken and Nancy were hoping they would be accepted for admission. Their tour of the Ped wing had convinced them the facility was the right place for him. Rusk challenged patients to focus all their energies on getting better within an atmosphere of teamwork that was reminiscent of the INN and actively inclusive of family, friends, and loved ones. It was precisely what the Trushes had been seeking for Daniel's rehabilitation.

In the end, their outlook may have been what tipped the scales in Daniel's favor. Daniel was in fragile shape, but the caseworkers decided the boy's innate tools and support system met their criteria well enough for them to take a chance.

The Trushes left Rusk feeling happy and excited. Daniel was ready to move on to the next phase of his recovery. Now they just had to wait for the staffs of Beth Israel and Rusk to coordinate his transfer.

The date they set for it was May 5, 1997.

CHAPTER NINE

For Ken and Nancy Trush, leaving Beth Israel with Daniel was a bittersweet occasion. They knew the hospital inside out. They'd fought many life-and-death battles alongside the doctors, nurses, therapists, and aides, and developed close, trusting relationships with them. It felt as if everyone there was a member of their extended family. The Trushes would miss them, miss their compassion, miss the feeling of being secure and protected in their expert hands. Miss the warm, healing environment Dr. Fred Epstein had created with his vision and humanity. But Daniel no longer needed the INN's acute care. It was time for the next leg of his journey.

The family orientation at Rusk would take up most of the day, and Ken and Nancy decided to keep Mike out of school so he could participate. That morning they had a brief assembly in the hospital playroom. In the grainy Polaroid photos, Danny is in a wheelchair, a strap around his head to keep it from sagging toward his chest. His trach hole is covered with gauze, the breathing tube capped. He is surrounded by his caretakers and the families of other kids the Trushes had gotten to know over the past two months.

When Daniel was ready to leave, they all hugged, kissed, took snapshots, and shed plenty of tears.

Then they said good-bye.

Daniel was placed on a gurney and then brought to a waiting ambulance. Ken, Nancy, and his younger brother joined him in the patient compartment, and they were off.

As they whisked down the East River Drive to Thirty-Fourth Street, Ken flashed back to that dreadful Sunday in March when Daniel had collapsed and they were sped to Beth Israel from the emergency room further downtown. He remembered the shrill wail of the sirens, how it had seemed to pierce straight through to his heart. It abruptly provoked a thought.

Crouched over Daniel, Ken looked into his wide-open eyes and asked if he'd like the driver to put on the siren. Danny smiled and blinked once. *Yes.* Ken leaned his head toward the front of the ambulance and made their request.

The driver agreed, hit the switch, and the vehicle's siren erupted into sound, lights flashing on its roof rack.

Ken rested back against the side of the ambulance and soaked in the moment. To him the blare of the siren was an exultant victory cry, asserting to the world that they'd made it. Daniel was alive in defiance of all odds, and they were moving into the future undaunted.

In his stretcher, Daniel had quietly understood, letting his father know with a smile.

The Trushes arrived at Rusk in under ten minutes and were brought straight up to the fifth floor—Daniel's new home, and in a true sense their entire family's new second home. An older facility than the INN, its more traditional hospital design initially struck Ken and Nancy as sterile and utilitarian, while the demeanor of its staff seemed professional but aloof. Where, they wondered, was the tight-knit family atmosphere? Didn't the doctors and nurses appreciate the ordeal they'd been through? The Trushes were jarred by the apparent difference.

After his check-in Daniel was brought into a special ward room with three or four beds reserved for the unit's most fragile kids. A large plate glass window in the dividing wall between the room and nurses' station allowed the nurses to keep a constant eye on their patients—and Daniel's bed was very tellingly situated nearest the wall, where it could be monitored extra closely.

With Daniel in his room, Rusk's intake staff gave Ken and Nancy their formal introduction to the facility, spelling out rules that put firm limits on the number of visitors who could be with Danny, as well as restrictions on actual visiting hours. The cutoff was 9 p.m. with no sleepovers by his parents. His therapists were going to work him hard, and he would need every available bit of rest to maintain his stamina.

The stipulations were something new to Ken and Nancy, and they deepened their unease. They'd started their around-the-clock watch at Beth Israel the day Danny was wheeled into the ICU. When he'd been moved into his private room, they'd expanded their routine to enable Ken to resume his duties at Agency and to accommodate a growing host of visitors. Every morning around 10:30, as Ken's overnight shift ended, groups of friends, family, and Dalton parents would come by and read to Daniel from books, newspapers, magazines, and any other material they could find. Then Nancy would arrive at noon or thereabouts— toward the end of Daniel's time at Beth Israel she'd gone back to teaching at Brick in the mornings—and stay until 7:00 or 8:00 at night. Mike had joined her after school let out in the afternoon, starting on his homework at the hospital. At 6:30 p.m., Ken would return from the office and have dinner with Mike and Nancy in Danny's room. Finally around 7:30 p.m., Nancy always took Mike home to finish his homework, relax, and prepare for bed, while Ken settled in to start the daily cycle over again.

But now the Trushes had to readjust. The first few nights at Rusk were the hardest on them. Danny was so frail and vulnerable it tore at their hearts to say good-bye. They would periodically call the nurses' station to ask how Danny was doing and sometimes tried to stay past visiting hours only to be reprimanded and sent home. Ken found it wrenching to return to their apartment and see his son's empty bed, an experience he hadn't grappled with while sleeping at his side for the past two months.

Within a few days, however, Ken and Nancy were able to figure out a new routine. Ken would drive to Rusk first thing in the morning so he could arrive at about 8:00 a.m., spend an hour with him, and then cab it over to Agency at 9:00 a.m. as Daniel's therapy promptly got underway. At 3:00 p.m., Nancy would pick Michael up from Dalton and ride the subway to the institute, stopping off for a quick bite to eat before heading upstairs to his brother's room. Ken tried to make it back by 7 p.m. and often jogged over from Agency's lower Manhattan headquarters, finding the two-mile run a good way for him to stay in shape and relieve stress. At first the whole family would stay with Daniel until visiting hours ended at 9:00 p.m. But as the pace of Mike's school year picked up, and his homework got heavier, Nancy would cab home with him at 8 o'clock most weeknights, with Ken staying the extra sixty to ninety minutes. Friday nights and weekends, the Trushes would leave for home together.

Ken and Nancy were careful to allocate time for the people who had stood by them for so long, their visits contributing to the warm, upbeat environment that had been an irreplaceable balm for Daniel in his most critical moments. Early on at Beth Israel the crushing news about his condition had cast a somber pall over their visitors. But Ken and Nancy's determination to fight for Danny, and nine-year-old Mike's uncomplaining acceptance of the dramatic changes in his own life—and his willingness to help his brother and parents in any way he could—had fostered the same accepting yet resolute spirit in their friends and loved ones. People understood what the Trushes were going through and knew their family needed support.

As the days and weeks passed, and Daniel had grown more stable, everybody settled into being themselves. Largely due to his uncles John and Steve, the hospital visits became almost like informal family gatherings, with plenty of upbeat conversation, joking, and laughter. When Daniel moved to Rusk, their uncle-versus-uncle act had come over with him, and as he grew more responsive, it never failed to make him laugh. But although it had been the norm at Beth Israel for people to drop in unannounced, Rusk's tighter policies made a visitation schedule necessary. Grandma Jeanne would take the train in from Queens two or three times a week. Grandma Eva, Pepe, and Nancy's sister Diane came to see Danny most days between 3:00 and 4:00 p.m., sometimes showing up ahead of Nancy and Michael with tasty home-cooked dinners and desserts. Tuesdays and Sundays were reserved for his vying uncles, his aunts Paula and Debbie—who brought their energy, funny stories and optimistic attitudes—and his cousins Lauren, Brittany, Bradley, Joanna, Matthew, and Liz. Ken and Nancy also made sure to coordinate regular visits for their friends, work colleagues, and Daniel's classmates.

Mother's Day fell on May 11. The whole family got together and turned the institute's playroom into a party room, everyone bringing food from home—enough for themselves and several other kids' relatives to enjoy.

During the celebration, Daniel seemed less alert than he'd been in his final days at Beth Israel. But it had only been a week since his transfer to Rusk, and Ken and Nancy hoped that it was a matter of adjusting to his new environment.

As he entered his second week of rehab, they would keep a watchful eye on him.

CHAPTER TEN

"Hi, Daniel! Y'know, you look like a Hollywood star!"

Daniel smiled. He didn't always when he heard that. Sometimes he'd show no reaction.

Standing beside Daniel's wheelchair, Ken smiled too. Jim, a senior citizen who did volunteer work at Rusk, said pretty much the same thing to Danny every morning. Armed with kindness, empathy, and humor, he enjoyed his role as a breeder of smiles for the Ped wing's young patients and their families.

"How you feeling today?" he asked, a small, round metal container in his palm.

The line was another reliable standby. Daniel smiled some more. So did his father. Then they waited as Jim opened his container and took out the host.

Ken had never asked Jim about his background. He may have been a retired priest. Or an extraordinary minister—a lay person that a priest or the hospital chaplain had authorized to administer the Eucharist to the sick. Regardless, his morning cheer, coupled with receiving Holy Communion, made for a wonderful, uplifting start to the day.

Two weeks into Daniel's stay at the institute, Ken especially appreciated the pick-me-up. His son's therapy wasn't going well. He was less responsive than at Beth Israel and often stared emptily into space. He had to be lifted into his wheelchair and couldn't sit up unaided; staffers would place folded towels under his head and arms to keep him from slumping downward. His muscles had badly atrophied, ruling out any but the most basic exercises. The therapists would stretch his arms, hands, legs, and feet to build up their strength and awaken his reflexes, but thus far he'd shown little improvement.

Ken and Nancy had quickly gotten past their first impression of the staff as professional but removed. They pushed their patients hard, and held their regimen to the exacting standards of a boot camp, but had shown Daniel steady compassion. Although it was an open question whether he could handle Rusk's demanding routine, no one at the facility was ready to concede defeat.

His parents would reject any suggestion that he couldn't make it. Everything they had gone through at Beth Israel had toughened them. They were almost defiant in their advocacy of their son, showing only resolve to his doctors and therapists. In their minds another facility wasn't an option.

But the mounting uncertainties around Daniel's rehab wore on them. He had already surpassed all expectations—could it be he'd hit a wall? Developed some medical complication? Or was he just exhausted? At the INN they had learned that recovery wasn't a steady press forward toward a goal line. Dr. Fred had seen it as cyclical, with ebbs and flows, lulls and seeming downturns. Was Daniel just going through a slow phase in the cycle?

They were questions without immediate answers. Whether or not things looked promising, the Trushes could only try to keep a tight hold on their faith and morale.

Right around this time, Ken started thinking about a story he'd read the previous Thanksgiving about a college student named Michael Segal, who sustained a gunshot wound to his head in a convenience store robbery. Although Ken had never dreamed it would eerily foreshadow what would happen to Daniel, the story had moved him close to tears.

Segal had stopped into the store to buy something the night of the holdup and been one of several victims shot in cold blood. He hadn't expected to make it through surgery, and even after he survived, he was left paralyzed and unable to speak. Some caregivers thought his neurological impairments would end his dream of graduating college and advised him to set more "realistic" objectives for his future. But there had been a particular doctor who gave him hope, suggesting he take it "one day at a time. For no matter how bad the situation looked, no one knew for certain what the brain could do."

Michael Segal would graduate the University of Texas with Phi Beta Kappa honors and a degree in social work, marry his high school sweetheart, and become a father. His own father had had a favorite maxim that he'd quoted throughout Segal's rehab and that Segal himself came to repeat on a daily basis: "Mile by mile, it's a trial; yard by yard, it's hard; but inch by inch, it's a cinch."

The saying had stuck in Ken's mind for months. He and Nancy would now adopt it for Daniel's therapy as the rehabilitation crawled through its laborious paces, using the other young man's story as an example of perseverance and eventual triumph.

But Ken quietly worried about his son. He'd endured so much, so many tests and life-threatening procedures. The move to Rusk had to be traumatic and confusing for him. Ken felt his heart break a little whenever he left his bedside.

It was during these first weeks of May that Ken composed his good-night song. He'd reached Daniel through music when he was comatose, playing the two Gloria Estefan ballads. This time he came up with a simple lullaby, praying it would soothe him and further his recovery:

I believe in you, yes I do.
No matter how long it takes.
I'll always be with you.

I love you,
I really mean these words.
I'm so proud of you.

You're doing so terrific,
Good night and God bless you.
I'll see you in the morning.

Each night before heading home, Ken offered Daniel his words and melody, tenderly encouraging him to sing along to its quiet strains. Music had helped work a miracle once before. Maybe it held enough power for another.

————————————

Dr. David Salsberg wore two hats. One was the plain psychologist's hat that he donned while giving support and counseling to his patients and their families at the Rusk Institute. The other was his pediatric *neuro*psychologist's hat, a fancier accessory sported only by the smaller club of experts qualified to evaluate children with brain injuries and plan out clinical strategies for their treatment.

In his more specialized capacity, Salsberg made assessments and reassessments spanning multiple therapeutic domains. He looked at a kid's functionality, attention span, and learning ability on admission to the institute and kept a close eye on things as rehab progressed. How well was the child healing? Did it appear his treatment had plateaued or was there a realistic shot at a higher ceiling? What were the best ways to address his current and future rehab therapies? His educational needs?

When Daniel Trush arrived at Rusk a couple of months after his traumatic brain injury—and just one month post-coma—his prognosis was cloudy. On the plus side, his records showed him to have been at a near-adult level of intelligence and cognition before his injury. He'd done well in school. You ran a checklist of a kid's strengths right off, and it would help if he'd been smart and motivated. But the deficits caused by Daniel's multiple strokes were severe. His body was badly wasted. He didn't necessarily look at you when you addressed him, and his responses to questions weren't always articulate or appropriate. It was difficult for Salsberg to predict where his therapy would go, and the kid admittedly looked down and out. But you never knew until you'd tried everything.

In his role as family counselor, Salsberg believed Daniel's parents were doing as well as anybody could. That was another positive. Coming over from an acute care hospital, nearly all families went through a shift from their fight, or survival, mode to one of having to grapple with their new, radically altered reality. When they feared their son or daughter was going to die, they had no time to think beyond the moment. But there was a tendency for parents to exhale after the crisis ended . . . a sense that they'd already fought their big fight, that the tough part was over.

Their relief was almost always fleeting. As the parents took stock, they realized life would never again be the same as it had been for the child—or for them. In the Ped wing it couldn't be pushed out of their awareness. They were on a floor full of kids in wheelchairs, and that cast an unsparing light on the formidable terrain ahead. It could be a hard landing for them.

NYU Langone was a teaching hospital, so almost every kid at Rusk was assigned an intern to manage his or her course of therapy. Daniel Trush's managing intern was a bright, energetic young woman named Jennifer Freiman Bender. Dr. Salsberg oversaw and guided Jennifer, often meeting with her and Daniel's family—and sometimes with all of them as a group. He, in turn, would regularly confer with Dr. Joan Gold, the institute's director of pediatric psychiatry. The constant interactions between the medical staff and rehab therapists produced a model of teamwork and mutual respect comparable to the INN's.

As a case supervisor, Salsberg would keep tabs on the progress of the child and his parents' mental and emotional state. With an injury as serious as Daniel's, he paid especially close attention. He would talk with Speech Therapy about how Daniel was communicating. He would talk to Physical Therapy about the best ways to position him for strength and range-of-motion exercises. He would ask Occupational Therapy what times of day the boy was most alert. These ongoing conferences occurred repeatedly during rounds, and Salsberg was always ready with his feedback and encouragement. A kid's status could change rapidly; he'd seen instances in which a patient was driven too hard and you had to back off, and others where a switch seemed to flip inside and you would witness a sudden, dramatic improvement. You had to take a nimble approach and be prepared to constantly revisit and rethink the recovery plan and its goals.

As Daniel underwent his first weeks of therapy with little to show for it, Salsberg would check in with Ken and Nancy

Daniel and Mike sharing a soda at an arcade about 1992.

The Trush family picking pumpkins in upstate New York around October, 1994, less than three years before Danny's injury.

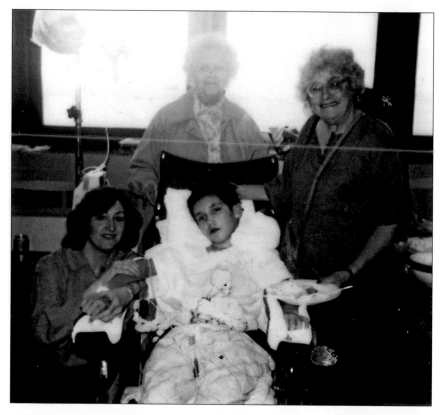

Nancy, Grandma Jeanne, and Grandma Eva with a worn-out Daniel at the Rusk Institute on Mother's Day 1997.

Dr. Epstein in his inner sanctum.

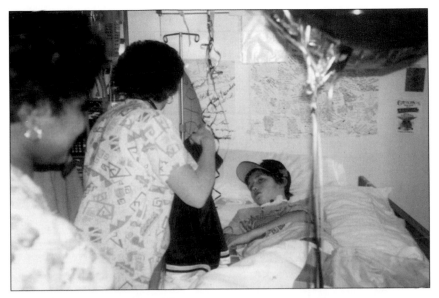

Daniel on his thirteenth birthday at Beth Israel, 1997.

Cousin Bradley, Daniel, and Mike with All-Star baseball player John Olerud during his August 1997 visit to the Rusk Institute.

Danny at St. Jean Baptiste Church for DMF's inaugural event, February 26, 2006.

Mike, Teddy Frischling, and Daniel at the annual Dribbl for a Cause fundraiser.

Daniel, Grandma Eva, Nancy (top row), Aunt Diane, and Grandpa Pepe (bottom) on vacation together in 2002.

Team Daniel at the New York City Marathon, 2007.

Kate Parkin pouring Danny a refreshment at the NYC Marathon.

Daniel and Mike crossing the Willis Avenue Bridge into the Bronx, near Mile 20 of the NYC Marathon.

Nancy, family, and friends awaiting Team Daniel with a chicken soup boost, NYC Marathon.

The Trush family at Mile 18 of the Marathon after chicken soup and hugs from Mom.

Team Daniel crossing the finish line of the New York City Marathon. Since Daniel was given a two-hour head start, his actual time was 7:46:12.

Mike and Daniel onstage with New York Yankees outfielder Nick Swisher, HOPE Week 2011.

DMF performing at the Brooks Atkinson Theater, HOPE Week.

Daniel and Mike onstage, HOPE Week.

DMF members assembled onstage, HOPE Week.

Aunt Debbie, Cousin Lauren, Uncle Steve, Cousin Bradley, and Cousin Liz

Back, left to right: Aunt Debbie, Nancy, Mike, Cousin Bradley, Cousin Liz, Uncle John, and Aunt Paula. Cousin Kaylin is in front.

DMF members performing the national anthem at Yankee Stadium, HOPE Week.

Daniel and Mike outside the Yankees dugout, HOPE Week.

The Trush family on the field at Yankee Stadium, HOPE Week.

DMF sings the national anthem prior to a New York Giants–New England Patriots preseason game, August 29, 2012.

to see how they were doing. They knew their son wasn't taking to Rusk's difficult regimen, and understood the staff was concerned it might be too much for him. But their patience and dedication didn't vacillate. Even when he seemed completely disconnected, they never spoke or acted as if he wasn't there. He was always made to be part of things.

That kind of supportiveness was important, and it wasn't exclusively reserved for Daniel. Salsberg had noticed that the love and support of his family members for each other was as unwavering as it was toward the boy. It was clear they all had their bad days. Ken and Nancy were always quick to state that they felt the same frustrations anyone else in their situation might experience. But they kept going. At the most elementary level, that was their strongest trait. They just kept going.

Yet Salsberg had remained on the lookout for signs they were headed for a crash. Daniel was having problems, serious ones, and there was no guarantee he would overcome them. While Ken and Nancy seemed solid as rock, they were under tremendous and constant pressure. His counselor's hat firmly on his head, Salsberg would make sure he continued checking in on them.

Even the steadiest rocks could be toppled, and the Trushes were only human.

———————————

After two weeks of basic massage and therapist-assisted stretching and range-of-motion exercises, Daniel was introduced to the tilt table. It was a painful, frightening, and necessary initiation.

People who are bedridden or confined to wheelchairs almost invariably develop problems related to their physical inactivity.

Muscles contract, leading to spasms that can be agonizing and violent. When this happens to joints *connected* by muscles, tendons, and ligaments, they also contract—or shorten—and inhibit even simple movements. The muscle contractures pull the bones into unnatural positions and weaken them so they become prone to fractures and osteoporosis. The spinal cord can bend out of shape and develop degenerative conditions. Prolonged immobility may cause pressure sores, put stress on the internal organs, lead to fluid buildup and infection in the lungs, hamper bowel function, and damage the circulatory, urinary, and renal systems.

For a person with normal use of his legs, standing itself is an important exercise. When someone stands erect, the simple downward pull of gravity will distribute his weight throughout his entire frame. This elongates the muscles, improves blood flow to the extremities, and increases bone density. No amount of therapeutic stretching and manipulation of the limbs can equal its widespread benefits.

The tilt table is a platform on a pivoted base that can be angled by degrees from a horizontal to an upright position. At Rusk, tilt-table therapy is the launch point for most kids suffering from whole or partial paralysis, a progressive step in their rehab after they've spent extended time being bedridden. A child undergoing tilt-table therapy is lain flat on his back atop the platform. Over a period of weeks he is inclined by his therapists until his body is reintroduced to being fully vertical. Weight resistance and breathing exercises are slowly incorporated into the thirty-minute sessions.

Daniel was one of the weakest kids at Rusk. He had no mobility and couldn't keep his head up straight. On his first day, he was placed on the platform and fastened to it with five restraining straps. There were separate straps for his head, chest, and waist, one across his knees, and one for his feet. That routine would become a regular part of his treatment. Often just semiawake, his level of awareness varying from session to session, he was confused about what was going on and would grow fearful and disoriented even when the therapists explained things to him. The boy was expending a great deal of his available energy climbing his way out of a hole that was fathoms deep. As David Salsberg would later note, that "drains attention, and attention is necessary for your short-term memory and for the ability to avoid being overwhelmed by your surroundings."

Every couple of days, Daniel's therapists would slightly graduate his vertical elevation, giving his physical systems the chance to readjust to working while he was upright. But even with a slow transition, it was unnatural to rise from a supine position without actively standing up. His inner ear would detect an involuntary tilt and transmit the information to his brain. His brain would interpret the data as his body falling off balance and send out panic signals.

Daniel would feel scared, helpless, and out of control. But if his anxiety and confusion were acute, his physical anguish was indescribably worse. He'd been reduced to sixty-five pounds. The pull of gravity on his long-dormant muscles was excruciating—and he couldn't always communicate it. His therapists would carefully watch his facial expressions, and listen to his vocalizations, for signs that he'd gone beyond his pain threshold. But it was hard to read him. He might or might not grimace or make a sound when something hurt.

Although the pediatric therapy room was off-limits to parents, Ken and Nancy were occasionally allowed in so they could gain a fuller understanding of Daniel's tilt-table rehab. They saw him cry more than once. Nothing communicated how he felt more clearly than his tears.

Daniel was scheduled for the tilt table almost every morning for the next nine months. Over time, his familiarity with it made him less fearful of his sessions.

But they still always felt like torture.

As Daniel entered June, he showed few signs of progress. Finding it hard to measure his incremental gains, Ken and Nancy were delighted when a visitor once noticed he could keep his head up against the back of his wheelchair without the folded towels. It was a reminder that Daniel was taking small steps forward all the time. *Little things that weren't so little.*

But Daniel's care providers at Rusk harbored concerns about his ability to make it there. He'd built up some physical strength, but not a whole lot. Nor were the doctors and therapists convinced his mental acuity was returning. He seemed disengaged much of the time. Although he occasionally mouthed a word or two, the words weren't always coherent. His answers sometimes didn't match the therapists' questions. The rehab team felt they weren't reaching him, not inside.

Early in the month, a pair of staff doctors met with Ken to briefly review Daniel's case. One gave him his read on Daniel's status, expressing the mounting uncertainty that he would draw substantial benefits from Rusk's aggressive rehab. The other doctor, a developmental geneticist, suggested that Ken and Nancy schedule cranial and upper body MRI exams—the latter because the most common location for aneurysms was the aorta, above the heart—for Michael and themselves. Since no one knew what had led Daniel's aneurysms to form, he wanted to see if they might have been inherited, and whether any of his immediate family members might be at risk. Ken recognized that taking the precautionary scans was a sensible measure. But it made him uneasy. What if they revealed Mike had an aneurysm? The doctors at the INN had said the odds were minuscule . . . but *what if?* The geneticist's suggestion also led him to wonder if he bore some unintentional responsibility for Daniel's injury . . . if he'd brought him pain and suffering by passing on the defect. The guilt accompanying that thought wasn't logical or rational. Still, it was there inside him. And he knew it would grow inside Nancy too.

Ken left the conversation feeling assaulted. He recalled having felt the same when he was told Daniel wouldn't survive his second night in the hospital, told he'd be in a permanent vegetative state, told he was probably blind. . . .

Those predictions had been wrong, every one of them, and he had to believe his son could defy expectations again. He thought Daniel was a little more alert than when he'd arrived at Rusk, but the signs were hard to pin down. It was a look in his eye here, a facial expression there. Ken would watch for them, as he'd watched for signs of life from Daniel on so many nights at Beth Israel, when it had been the two of them, the machines, and the music that had temporarily masked their sounds. Danny had come a long way, and Ken was inexpressibly grateful for it. But he wondered if the doctors and therapists could be convinced.

He always wished he could stay the night with his son. He hated walking out the door. The resistance pulling him back to Daniel's bedside was hard to overcome. It was like being caught in a lasso.

One night, Ken was alone with Daniel at the end of a long day of rehab, getting ready to leave with the conclusion of visiting hours. Nancy and Mike had already cabbed uptown to their apartment so Mike could finish his homework and go to bed.

Ken leaned over Daniel to sing his good-night song. Taking hold of his hand, he began, "I believe in you—"

"Doop . . . doop."

Ken's eyes widened slightly. He looked at the boy's face a second before starting the next line. Then went on, "Yes, I do."

Another moment passed. Ken waited.

"Doop, doop," Daniel offered in the barest of whispers . . . and smiled.

Now Ken was smiling too. "I'll always be with you," he sang.

"Doop, doop . . . doop."

Ken was grinning outright now. If he'd come to rely on anything these past few months, it was Daniel's ability to surprise people. But his son riffing with him on his lullaby . . . that had even caught him off guard.

"I love you," he sang, and waited for a response.

But Daniel just smiled drowsily. All at once he seemed very tired.

Ken wasn't going to push. Cupping his hand over Daniel's head, he bent closer and finished the song by himself. Then he kissed the boy good-night, waved to the nurses on the other side of the glass window, and strode out toward the elevators.

I believe in you. Doop, doop. Yes, I do. Doop, doop. I'll always be with you. Doop, doop, doop . . .

The newly reworked and expanded good-night song kept playing in Ken's mind throughout his drive home. He loved his collaboration with Daniel. But his goal-oriented mind already saw ways to make it better.

They had only gotten as far as the first verse, after all.

"Itcheo," Danny said in the faintest of whispers.

This was Friday evening, a few days after he'd joined in on the good-night song. Ken, Nancy, and Mike were in his ward room as visiting hours wrapped up, preparing to leave together as they always did on weekends. Daniel's contributions to the song's lyrics—"doop" and "yeah"—had started him vocalizing, and David Salsberg and his staff had quickly taken notice. It didn't mean their concerns about his ability to handle Rusk had gone by the wayside. Daniel remained paralyzed and continued to receive most of his nourishment through a feeding tube. He still seemed detached, and his voice hadn't returned. But his whispered singing was as good as a shout insofar as declaring that he was mentally present. Salsberg was encouraged things might work out.

Now Mike's eyes studied his parents from behind his big round glasses. They'd turned back toward his older brother.

"What did you say, Daniel?" Nancy asked.

"Itcheo . . ."

Nancy gave Ken a questioning glance. He shrugged his own puzzlement, then looked at Danny. "Itch-eo?" he said, making sure they were hearing him correctly.

"Itcheo," Daniel repeated a third time.

A moment went by. Nancy's forehead creased in thought. "Daniel, do you mean itchy?"

"Right . . ." Danny whispered.

"Right!" Nancy repeated excitedly. "Itcheo means *itchy*!"

"Danny," Ken said, "where do you feel itchy?"

"Right . . ."

Ken was confused. It occurred to him that Daniel still might be answering their first question. "Can you tell us where you're feeling itch—?"

"Right side!" Nancy blurted out. "Do you mean you're itchy on the *right side?*"

Daniel blinked once in the affirmative.

Nancy and Ken both smiled. Mike smiled too, his face crinkling with happiness.

"Where on the right side, Danny?" Ken asked.

"Face," Daniel struggled to whisper.

Nancy moved close against the bed and started scratching his right cheek. "Is this the spot?"

"Higher."

She scratched higher up toward his cheekbone. "Is this it?"

"Lower."

She scratched lower down toward his jaw. "This?"

"Higher," Daniel replied. Then added, "Eye."

"Oh," Nancy said. "It's itchy up by your *eye!*" She raised her hand up near near his eye, scratched. "Is it here?"

"Lower."

She scratched under his eye. "Here?"

"Higher."

"*Here?*"

"Right . . ."

Nancy frowned. "I can't find the spot where he's itchy," she said.

Ken was already at the bed. He scratched slightly to the right of where Nancy had been doing it. "How's this feel, Danny?"

A brief silence. Then Daniel whispered, "Lower . . . right."

Ken paused. It was maddening. How could they keep missing the spot?

He was struggling to come up with an answer for himself when Nurse Helen poked her head into the ward. "Excuse me, but visiting hours have ended," she said.

Ken and Mike stiffened as Nancy turned toward the entryway. Nurse Helen was very strict. But Nancy's friendly, easygoing manner had a way of softening her up.

"Thank you," Nancy said with a smile. "We're just saying good-night."

Nurse Helen peered in at her a moment, then snapped her a nod and left the entry. Ken hurriedly got back to scratching Daniel's face. *Under his eye, further to the right, but lower than before . . .*

"Higher," Daniel said.

Ken stood there at a complete loss. They were pressed for time.

"Let me give it another try," Nancy said, leaning forward. "Daniel, how about here . . . ?"

"Ahhh," Daniel exhaled with relief.

Ken looked at Nancy. He wanted to hug her.

"Does that feel better, Daniel?" she asked, scratching away.

"Ahhhhhhhh," he exhaled more deeply.

Ken's eyes lit with pure delight. He could have lived his whole life waiting for those sighs . . . although he still didn't understand why it had taken so long to quiet Danny's itch. His face only had so many places to scratch, and they'd been at it for a good ten minutes. They *had* to have hit the right area on one of their earlier tries, hadn't they?

He was still pondering things when Nurse Helen reappeared in the entryway.

"I'm sorry," she said, "you really will have to leave now."

This time Ken and Nancy nodded without a word, gesturing for Mike to hop off his chair. Rules were rules for a reason, and the nurse had already bent them once. The kids in the ward needed their rest.

Besides, Ken thought, how were they supposed to explain they only wanted to stick around long enough for one more "Ahhhhhhhh"?

"I love you," Ken quietly intoned.

"Yeah . . . yeah . . . yeah," Daniel whispered.

"I really mean these words."

"Yeah . . . yeah, yeah."

"I'm soooo proud of you."

"Yeah . . . yeah, yeah."

"You're doing so terrific."

"Thanks, thanks . . . thanks."

Ken was pleased. He'd encouraged the boy to go on contributing to his song, waiting after every line, and Daniel had responded with more whispered lyrics. Like the song's first verse, its second had turned into an answering duet, and Ken hadn't missed the "thanks" in direct response to his praise. Danny had only mouthed basic sounds—the "doop-doops"—when he'd tacked on to the words before. He was now using real words, and appropriate ones. For Ken nothing showed more clearly that he could understand the *meaning* of the song.

Ken kissed Daniel on his cheek and left. It was now the middle of June. His family's MRIs were scheduled for the following week.

Daniel's "itcheo" episodes recurred often after the first one. Sometimes his face itched him, sometimes his back or shoulders . . . and the elusive itch could move around. His parents might scratch for half an hour at a time before they found the spot that was bothering him and were rewarded with a long, precious sigh of relief. Ken had begun to think the itches might be related to his son's body waking up little by little, his skin and nerve endings coming alive to sensory input on scattered channels. He also suspected part of it was just Daniel enjoying his and Nancy's loving touch as feeling and sensation returned to his body. Nobody could say for sure.

Meanwhile, Daniel's voice hadn't returned. Its disappearance after he'd left Beth Israel was a mystery. The caregivers at Rusk knew he'd started using words to communicate with his parents back in April. The INN's medical team had removed his tracheotomy tube in the expectation that he would talk more easily—and often—without the tube obstructing his vocal cords. Daniel's whispered "itcheos" and running collaboration with his father on the good-night song showed that he was becoming more engaged. But in his solitary moments, Ken wondered if he'd ever hear his son talk again.

Ken, Nancy, and Michael took their MRIs on June 23, a few days after Mike's school let out for summer recess. Their tests were all negative, showing no malformations or weaknesses of any kind in their blood vessels. The biggest relief for Ken and Nancy, of course, was when Mike came away with a clean bill of health. But each had worried about the other's feelings of guilt over possibly being the one to have passed along the defect. The results eliminated that irrational but nonetheless real pressure from their minds.

The Trushes would never know what brought about Danny's aneurysms. The most common risk factors, like smoking, heavy drinking, and street drug use, didn't apply in his case. In the end medical science would simply mark them as random occurrences.

Years later, Ken and Nancy would come to believe the explanation might have been something beyond the medical—that what happened was part of God's plan for Daniel and themselves. But in late June 1997, they were just happy to have the tests out of the way so they could focus on helping their oldest son get better.

CHAPTER ELEVEN

As Manhattan stewed under an early July heat wave, the halls at Rusk had grown quieter. Sundays were slow, with only group recreational therapy sessions on the schedule, and Daniel was too weak to participate in them. Many of the Trushes' friends and relatives had taken their vacations, leaving him with fewer visitors. School had let out, and kids were involved in their summer activities. There were only two comments in Daniel's online guestbook that month, both from the same classmate. He hadn't been forgotten. But life went on.

Even Michael would be leaving the city for several weeks. With his MRI out of the way, Ken and Nancy had concluded it would be good for him to have a break. They'd originally planned for him and Daniel to attend sleepaway camp together, and now they decided to go ahead and send him on his own so he could have some measure of normalcy restored to his life. Michael had spent nearly every night for the past three months in hospital rooms and had done more than simply adapt and accept it—he'd shown a compassion beyond his age to his brother and other sick kids.

When Daniel got to Rusk, Mike had been quick to take some of the younger patients under his wing, even though he wasn't much more grown up in years than they were. One wheelchair-bound little boy, Jorge, had come in for a corrective procedure on his legs. Only four years old, he needed help cutting his food, and Mike would assist him with it during dinner. Another boy named Chris had cerebral palsy and was almost entirely unable to talk. He had an electronic toy that could speak a few phrases, and Mike's goal each day was to make him laugh by playfully imitating what the machine was saying. He seemed to respond to that and often let out a big laugh.

And then there was Terrence, who was about Mike's age. His spinal injury had left him with no use of his legs and with limited use of his arms and hands. His face all chubby brown cheeks, he wore round wire glasses and needed a chest brace to hold him in his wheelchair. Terrence didn't always get along well with the rest of the kids, and he could be pushy toward the smaller ones. He'd cut in front of them when they lined up to use the toys and games, blocking them out with his wheelchair instead of waiting his turn. Mike had seen him misbehave and start arguments. Although he usually settled down once he got the therapists' attention, it took a lot of cajoling before he would cooperate with them.

With the other kids Mike could hang out in the playroom, just being a pal, listening and talking to them over video games and pizza. But he was a little reticent about playing with Terrence. He didn't understand why he carried on so often.

Now Mike would be leaving for camp with mixed feelings. Before Daniel's injury, he'd looked forward to that summer being their first away together. He tended to be shy and quiet around other kids and had counted on his older brother showing him the ropes. Instead he'd have to go it alone. He was excited about the athletic activities—especially the outdoor stuff like hiking and canoeing—and had been prepared to do them without Daniel for weeks. But it was still disappointing to know that Danny wouldn't be with him.

On June 29 Michael had left for Camp Wildwood, in Bridgton, Maine. Several of Daniel's friends from Dalton were there, and they did their best to help him get acclimated to his new surroundings. Still, Michael was anxious about his brother. He'd seemed to be getting stronger. But despite his young age, Mike had already learned a hard lesson about life: It could spin you around in a dizzying circle without warning.

He would think about Daniel constantly in his weeks away at camp.

———————————

Back in New York, meanwhile, things hadn't changed much for Daniel. He wasn't talking and remained very weak.

Ken was alone with Danny one hot night when the aides arrived to bathe him. The task required three nurses and aides. Unable to sit erect or hold his head up straight without the back of a wheelchair for support, Daniel was cleaned while lying in a mesh gurney.

The hospital staffers would remove his gown, cover him with towels, then transfer him onto the gurney and wheel him out past the nurses' station into a shower room with several stalls. Ken always gave them a hand if he was present. He'd help lift his son onto the gurney or hold it steady as they put him on the mesh sling. Then he'd go into the shower room with them.

Ken did exactly that that night. The largest stall had been designed to accommodate a gurney, and Ken waited as the aides pushed Daniel into it and turned on the water.

The moment it touched him, he started to cry. Ken tensed. The mix was too cold. Daniel was all skin and bones. The spray wouldn't have had to be freezing to feel like a thousand pinpricks on his body.

Standing helplessly outside the shower stall, Ken heard his son exclaim in a voice that was simultaneously recognizable and unfamiliar: *"It's coooold."*

Ken didn't know what to think or feel. Daniel had spoken in a high boy's voice before his injury and then afterward at Beth Israel. But the voice that had pushed up through his tears now was *deep*. It was disconcerting. Surreal. Like something from the movie *The Exorcist*.

"It's cooold," Daniel repeated.

Ken teetered between joy and shock. He'd been hoping and praying to hear Daniel's voice for weeks. But this was a different one than he'd ever known or expected

His son didn't sound anything like his son. Yet it *was* Daniel. Daniel speaking, finally. With the low-pitched voice of a man.

Joy and shock.

His mind in turmoil, Ken peered into the shower stall, trying to make sense of what he was hearing. Then a realization overtook him: Daniel had gone through puberty. He was thirteen years old. His body had been maturing, probably even while he was comatose. Its atrophied condition had either delayed his hormonal growth spurts or made them outwardly unnoticeable. And he'd been silent when the changes deepened his voice.

Ken had just long enough to take that in when the aides turned off the water and covered his son in towels again, wrapping one around his head like a turban. As they rolled Daniel out of the shower room, he kept talking in his new voice. Ken wasn't sure for how long. Keeping pace with the gurney, he was talking too, answering Danny. He didn't know what either of them said. He was so flustered, he wouldn't be able to remember.

As soon as they were back in the ward, with Daniel dressed and under his bed sheets, Ken called Nancy at home. His shock had subsided a bit. Now he only wanted her to hear their son talk— and wanted to prepare her for it.

His voice trembling with excitement, Ken gave her a summary of everything that had happened, then held the receiver up to Danny's ear.

"It's Mom," he said. "Say hello!"

He looked up at Ken from his pillow but didn't say anything.

"Danny," Ken said, "it's your mother!"

Daniel was silent.

Ken waited. "Don't you want to say 'hi'?" he said after a few seconds.

Daniel said nothing.

Ken raised the handset back to his lips.

"What's going on, Ken?"

"Nancy," he said. "Daniel was *talking*."

"In that low voice."

"Right," Ken said. "But he isn't talking now."

"What did he say?" Nancy asked. "When he was talking, I mean?"

"'It's cold.'"

"That's all?"

"No. He said that a few times. Then he said something else to me. And I said something back to him." He paused. "And we talked to each other."

"For how long?"

"I don't know." Ken was momentarily quiet again. He was wondering what about the cold water hitting Daniel had finally gotten him to speak. "Two or three minutes in the shower and hallway. Then maybe thirty seconds here in his room."

"And you don't know what either of you said?"

"No," he replied. What *had* brought his son's voice back? "I don't."

Nancy hesitated at the other end of the line. She'd noticed his absent tone. "Ken?"

"Yes . . . ?"

"Are you feeling okay? Maybe you should come home ..."

He glanced over at Daniel. His eyelids looked heavy. It was getting late. Almost time for the good-night song.

"I'm fine," he said truthfully. "I'm leaving soon."

Ken hung up the telephone, thinking. A boy's vocal cords and larynx grew in size during puberty—and grew fast. That was what made the voice drop in pitch. With his vocal cords suddenly developed, Daniel might have been too weak to force enough breath over them to make them work. But the cold shower spray had been a jolt to his system, bringing a burst of air up into his throat and voice box. When the adrenaline rush dissipated, his strength had fled with it.

It seemed a logical guess anyway. But whatever the explanation, Ken had no doubt in his mind that Danny would speak again. He'd done it at Beth Israel, and now he'd broken through at Rusk. He would keep at it.

Ken wondered how he might be able to help him.

As July wore on, Ken and Nancy tried to make the best of their summer weekends by taking Daniel for neighborhood outings in his wheelchair. Sometimes they would head over to a nearby pet store and play with the puppies. Every once in a while they'd go out to Baskin-Robbins, treating Danny to selections he could easily swallow and digest, like a vanilla milk shake or strawberry ice cream. For Ken and Nancy, these respites were the equivalent of vacation getaways.

With its trees, playgrounds, and ball fields, St. Vartan Park was only a block or so uptown and seemed another good destination. But a stroll there had to be aborted when the battering heat made Danny noticeably uncomfortable.

Where else could they go to escape the sweltering temperatures? What did anyone in the city do? Ken and Nancy wondered about a movie. Daniel loved big budget adventure films, and *Batman & Robin* was showing at a nearby theater. A wheelchair-accessible, *air-conditioned* theater. Was it doable?

Daniel's therapists saw no problem with the idea, and Ken and Nancy brought him to a Sunday matinee. But a few minutes into the opening sequence, his face twisted up, and he burst into tears.

"Danny . . . what's wrong?" Ken asked.

He kept crying.

Nancy dried his tears with a tissue. "Is the movie too loud?" she said. "Is that it, Daniel?"

He blinked once for yes. At times it was still easier for him to use the code than his voice. The movie's high-decibel sound system was too much for him to take.

His upset parents hurriedly left the theater with him. Back at Rusk afterward, they were told a hypersensitivity to louder sounds was known to sometimes occur with head traumas. The condition often involved damage to the auditory nerve, but that wasn't always the case. Hearing was a complex and only partially understood process. The condition might pass, or Daniel's tolerance might increase with simple exposure. Because his trip to the movies had been the first since his injury, the therapists suggested that Ken and Nancy cautiously give it another try.

They did so about ten days later. *Men in Black* was at the same multiplex that had been running the Batman sequel, and they brought Daniel to see it equipped with cotton and plugs for his ears.

Things worked out better than the time before. Danny was able to stay through the movie's first half hour before the volume started bothering him. Leaving the theater, Ken and Nancy were satisfied he'd enjoyed being able to watch Agents J and K tackle dangerous extraterrestrials for a short time.

Better was better, and progress was progress.

The song on the boom box was the old sixties rock hit "Under the Boardwalk." Ken turned toward Daniel as the bass guitar played its climbing introduction, a triangle and güiro giving accent to the languid rhythm.

"Ready, Dan?" he asked. Looking up at him from the bed, Daniel's eyes said he was.

Johnny Moore's smooth, rich voice was coming from the box now. Ken and Daniel listened to him sing about the sun beating down and burning the tar up, and your shoes getting so hot you wished your tired feet were fireproof under the boardwalk . . .

"Ooooooooo-ooooooooo-oooooo," Ken joined in with the backing harmonies, doing his best to stay in tune with their elongated phonetic sounds.

Quietly, Daniel echoed him: "Ooooooooo-ooooooooo-oooooo . . ."

Ken managed to smile and keep singing. His son's new voice was a bullfroggy croak. Nothing could have been sweeter to his ears.

A week had passed since the night Daniel was shocked into talking in the shower. As Ken had started thinking about ways to give him back his voice, his mind had naturally turned to music. In the Rusk's Ped wing, the speech therapists worked on breathing exercises with kids to improve their vocal function, encouraging them to produce sounds with the air flowing up from their chests to their throats. The exercises were reminiscent of the ones that professional singers did when they warmed up before performances. The biggest difference seemed to be that the singers would usually run through musical notes or scales.

Danny had responded to music before. It had stimulated his awareness, relaxed and activated different parts of his mind. But that only described a small part of its healing power. As close a bond as Ken had always enjoyed with him, the music that had surrounded their long nights together since his injury had forged an even stronger father-son connection, one that had flourished on entirely new, deeper levels. Most of all, however, it seemed to have been the path by which Daniel's very *soul* had emerged from the prison of his comatose body on that special Easter Sunday—that holy day of transcendence and renewal— three months before.

Might combining music with the speech exercises now work to restore his voice?

Ken had wanted to find out. Just as he'd done at Beth Israel with the Gloria Estefan CDs, he started playing Daniel early rock numbers during his nightly visits—midtempo tunes by groups like The Drifters, The Four Seasons, and Gene Chandler "The Duke of Earl," with flowing, soulful melodies and richly layered singing parts. Echoing their ooos, ahhs, and other phonetic background vocals, he'd urged Daniel to join in with him.

Daniel had immediately responded by shaping the vocals with his lips. Ken had seen the effort on his face as he'd pulled up the breath to get sound out of them, *dredged* up the breath—and then seen satisfaction overspread his features when he'd rattled out his first notes.

They'd been singing to the music every night since. And every night, Danny's voice had gotten stronger.

Now the Drifters' lead singer was wistfully recalling the sound of the carousel, the taste of hot dogs and French fries, and being on a blanket with his baby.

"Mmmmmm-mmmmm . . ." Ken sang along, his lips pursed to mimic the backing vocals.

"Mmmmmm-mmmmm . . ." Daniel harmonized rustily.

Ken had no illusions about his own vocal abilities. He liked to joke that his range was half an octave. On his best days. But singing with Daniel in that little ward room, filled with pride for him, he knew he could have repeated their performance on every rooftop and street corner in New York City—on a Broadway stage even—without a hint of self-consciousness.

It simply felt that good.

It was the third Sunday in July. The urban heat and mugginess had hung on. Outside Rusk's walls the air felt like a moist sponge. With heavy rainstorms threatening, Daniel's small group of visitors had gone home, wishing him and his parents an early good-night.

Ken and Nancy didn't mind the extra time to themselves. They were preparing to phone Michael at camp. Whenever they spoke to him, the first thing he did was ask about his brother. While they always told him Danny was doing okay, they'd sensed his quiet unease over the past couple of weeks. Mike was smart and insightful. He would know they'd filter whatever they told him. He'd seemed to constantly have his antennas raised for any clues that they were holding back. He needed something definitive and concrete, and deserved to know about the recent development.

Ken dialed the camp director's number, waited. Sitting on the edge of Daniel's bed, Nancy was anticipant. They'd talked about making this call for days.

The director picked up after a few rings, and Ken asked to speak with Mike.

Michael was in the cafeteria having dinner with his group when the camp director entered and then walked over to his table. His parents had phoned from New York, the director said.

Mike instantly grew worried. He'd spoken to his mother and father since coming to camp, but there were set hours for family calls—and this wasn't one of them. Could something have happened to Daniel? He had seemed to be holding steady when Mike last saw him a few weeks ago. Mike had had a lot of fun in that time, but never without feeling bad that his brother was in a hospital bed and unable to enjoy it. He prayed he was all right.

The director's office was in the main lodge—the same building as the cafeteria. He told Mike he could take the call there.

Mike got up and left with him, his dinner half eaten. At the table, his friends' normally raucous conversation became muted. One of the other boys had a sister who'd been a classmate of Danny's, and he knew how sick Daniel was. In fact, he and his sister were frequent visitors to the online guestbook. His concerned, watchful eyes followed Mike to the door.

"Hello?" Michael said.

As he'd walked the long length of the cafeteria, then out onto the front porch, he had felt as if he was moving through wet concrete. Had something happened to Daniel? What if he never saw his older brother again? Never spoke to him again or had a chance to tell him how much he loved him? It had been his greatest dread before leaving home, and suddenly he'd been terrified that the nightmare might have come true. Part of him knew Daniel would have wanted him to go off to camp. Would have told him to go if he could talk. But he still felt guilty. Like he'd abandoned Danny.

His heart slamming in his chest, praying nothing had happened to his brother, Mike had turned on the porch, then gone through the separate entrance to the director's office. He'd only gotten more scared and nervous when his eyes fell on the telephone receiver. It had sat on the desk as if just waiting there for him to pick it up.

Now Mike held the receiver against his cheek, his small fingers tightly wrapped around it. He could hear the loud rush of his own pulse as he listened for an answer. It was like being inside a wind tunnel.

"Hi, Mike," someone finally replied at other end of the line.

Mike stood with his mouth frozen open for a full thirty seconds. He might have jumped off his feet but was too stunned to move a muscle. He'd known his caller at once. His voice was strange . . . kind of. Deep. But he'd probably have known who it was if he'd growled at him like a bear.

"Daniel!" he exclaimed, and then just held the phone in silence again. He was too amazed to say another word, but that was all right.

He'd already said the only one that counted.

CHAPTER TWELVE

It was just after 9:30 p.m., a weeknight in the third week of July. Nurse Helen had made her crisply punctual appearance to remind Ken that visiting hours were over. He'd given her a nod, popped his oldies CD out of the boom box, and leaned over the bedside, bringing his face so close to Daniel's that the tips of their noses almost touched.

"I believe in you," he sang.

"Doop, doop," Daniel joined in.

"Yes, I do."

"Doop, doop."

"No matter how long it takes."

"Doop, doop, doop."

"I'll always be with you."

"Doop, doop, doop."

Ken paused. He'd almost gotten used to the throaty croak that was Daniel's new voice. He had been using it spottily but a little more each day, though it was easier for him on some of those days than others. On Sunday he'd gotten winded just saying hi to Mike over the phone, and Ken had brought the receiver away from his ear so he could catch his breath. He'd done the same thing now, giving Daniel a chance to rest.

After a moment or two Daniel looked ready. Ken picked up on the lyrics.

"I love you."

"Yeah, yeah, yeah."

"I really mean these words."

"Yeah, yeah, yeah."

"I'm soooo proud of you."

"Yeah, yeah, yeah."

Ken launched into the next and last verse without a break. Daniel had seemed to get stronger as he was singing, and he thought he'd extend his vocal and mental workout.

"You're doing so terrific," he went on.

"Thanks, thanks, thanks."

"Good night and God bless you."

"Yeah, yeah, yeah."

Now Ken did pause again, although it was his turn to sing, *I'll see you in the morning*. Daniel had added two lines to the verse—repeating the word *thanks* three times, then *yeah* three times between Ken's existing lines. But it had been Daniel who'd ended each of the previous verses. Ken wanted to see if it was just a coincidence or if his son grasped the pattern and would come up with one more line to round it off

"I'll see you in the morning," he sang at last. And then waited before giving Daniel his usual kiss on the cheek. He was still leaning over the bed, close, close, looking expressively down into his eyes, practically trying to will him into knowing what he wanted him to do.

Daniel's looked back up at him in silence for several seconds. Then, slowly, he sang, "Hopefully . . . hopefully . . . hopefully."

Ken's eyebrows lifted with surprise. "Hopefully?"

Daniel grinned slyly at him. Then Ken grinned too. A big, amused grin. The boy had been through hell—and then some. But his sense of humor really was none the worse for wear.

Hopefully, to be sure.

Daniel had finally given the good-night song its ending— and a proper one at that.

———

"Suzeenah . . . War . . . rior . . . Princess," Daniel announced.

Susan Guzzardo chuckled from the entryway. In the ward room, Ken and Nancy were also laughing. In her eighth year as a pediatric therapist at Rusk, the energetic brunette had in part earned her nickname with Daniel because of her persistence and drive advancing his rehab. But it really had more to do with Conan the Barbarian.

As Daniel used his voice more often, it had become evident his injury had resulted in a condition called dysarthria—the slurred or slow speech frequently associated with stroke victims. The neurological damage Daniel suffered had weakened the muscles of his face and mouth, and that had led to difficulties speaking and swallowing. His therapists also suspected impairment of his short-term, or working, memory—task-related memories that normally weren't stored in the brain for more than a few hours. When a kid remembers how to get dressed, or his favorite foods, it involves long-term memory. When he recalls where he's hung his coat at a friend's house, or what he was served for lunch in the school cafeteria, it's a short-term memory.

Guzzardo had sought to address Daniel's issues with drills that would simultaneously strengthen his vocal mechanisms and improve his short-term memory retention. Children with motor disorders were her particular field of expertise, and she knew the textbook exercises that were physically and neurologically effective. But she also inherently understood that keeping a child engaged was half the battle. Whenever possible, she would tailor the demanding, repetitive drills to a kid's imagination so they would be less monotonous.

Her Conan the Barbarian drill had rapidly become one of Daniel's favorites. Repeating the famous line from the Arnold Schwarzenegger movie was perfect for putting his memory and vocal system through their paces. And he got a kick out of doing it—especially when he had an audience.

"What is best in life?" Guzzardo said now. The setup line she'd borrowed from the film was mostly what had inspired the Warrior Princess moniker.

"To crush . . . your . . . enemies, see them . . . driven . . . before you . . ."

Daniel had trailed off into silence. Guzzardo and his parents waited, their eyes beaming encouragement. His features had tightened with the effort of pulling the rest out of his archived memories. Finally he nodded, as if to reassure himself he'd hauled it in.

"And hear the *lam* . . . *en* . . . *tation* . . . of . . . their women," he said, punctuating the sentence with a grin.

Suzeenah the Warrior Princess, and everyone else in the room, broke into smiles, cheers, and applause.

Progress.

———————

On the last weekend in July, Ken drove up to Maine to bring Michael home from camp. The break had been good for him, but he'd missed his family. After everything Daniel had been through since March, their month-long separation had felt interminable.

Although hearing Danny on the phone had relieved some of Mike's worries, he was eager to visit his older brother.

Ken left the city Friday afternoon and stayed overnight near Bridgton, returning with Mike the next afternoon.

Mike felt overjoyed to be back together with Daniel. Seeing firsthand how much he'd improved made his heart soar. Deep voice and all—Mike did tell him he sounded kind of creepy— he could *talk!*

The happiness over Mike's return wasn't confined to Daniel's room. Jorge, Chris, and the other kids brought the party into the playroom, where Mike would soon get back to combating alien invaders in video games between demonstrations of balloon volleyball and sponge bowling.

But one boy in Pediatrics wouldn't have long to celebrate before he made his wrenching good-bye.

One afternoon Nancy heard Terrence crying in the hallway outside Daniel's room. It didn't sound anything like the frustrated outbursts he'd sometimes have when being admonished for misbehavior. His deep, hitching sobs were pure sadness.

She went to the door and looked.

Along with several adult family members, the discharge team was gathered around his wheelchair—nurses, aides, and one of the therapists, Lisa Del Guidice. Lisa was responsible for programming all the recreational activities, and her warmth and close attention to each of her young patients made her a universally beloved member of the staff. She would schedule group music and art sessions, bring in therapy dogs for the kids to pet, invite clowns to entertain them with jokes and magic tricks, get them to build puzzles or color with crayons in the play room . . . whatever it took to keep them stimulated and engaged.

Now Lisa was walking along with Terrence, speaking to him gently as they wheeled him toward the elevators.

"I don't want to leave," he wept, tearing in a breath. *"I don't want to go back to the apartment!"*

Nancy felt the inside of her throat thicken. Kids were discharged from Rusk for different reasons. Often they reached a stage where they could derive the same benefits from outpatient therapy as they would staying on as inpatients. But sometimes the reason wasn't pretty. Sometimes a family's insurance just ran out.

Nancy didn't know why Terrence was being released. But it made her sad to realize he would have rather stayed at the hospital than go home. And what sort of home must it be for him to cry such bitter tears over going back? Nancy had never seen much of his family—he'd gone for weeks at a stretch without company. And he'd always been so needy, so desperate for attention. Rusk may have been the one place he'd felt accepted and cared for.

Nancy stood in the doorway as Terrence's wheelchair was pushed around a corner to an elevator bank and out of sight. She could hear the boy's cries trailing down the hall.

"I don't want to leave."

The incident was still weighing heavily on her when she told Ken about it later on. As Nancy described the pain she'd witnessed on Terrence's face, she again had to ask herself what problems he was facing outside the institute's walls.

Nancy and Ken couldn't get Terrence's heartbreaking departure out of their minds. They knew he wasn't the only kid with infrequent visitors. There were far too many of them. And the neglected ones weren't alone in dealing with loneliness and alienation. Even with the best support system, it would be hard for a disabled kid—or anyone with a disability, regardless of age—to go through life without a place of acceptance, a place where he didn't feel isolated, where the clock wasn't ticking against him.

Ken and Nancy discussed the subject into the night and on subsequent days and nights as well. If such a place actually existed, and people just paid what they could afford to come through its doors . . . if it could be a *home* . . . what sort of difference would it make in their lives?

Whenever they thought about Terrence, they had to wonder.

Little Billy had a halo. It was attached to his forehead with a pair of titanium screws.

One of the youngest and smallest of the young patients at Rusk, Little Billy was a charmer. With his dark brown hair, large almond-colored eyes, and precocious smile, he'd roll his wheelchair into Daniel's room during visiting hours and declare with a mild Hispanic accent, "Nurse Helen, Nurse Helen, Daniel is *out of control*."

Part of the gag was that all the kids in Ped knew Nurse Helen was very strict. Although Nancy's easygoing, friendly manner had softened her up a bit, she made everyone, parents and kids alike, adhere to the rules. Not that Danny was a problem. He always was quiet and polite, thanking everybody for the smallest things they did for him.

Which was why Little Billy thought it was so hysterically funny to shout what he did about Daniel.

Now, Ken and Nancy laughed at his tag line, and he giggled brightly along with them, a delighted look on his face. They weren't sure what had put him in a wheelchair. But they knew his halo—a circular metal brace with a kind of framework running down to a hard plastic vest over his shoulders—was used to stabilize the neck and head for patients with spinal injuries and diseases.

Little Billy enjoyed basking in the spotlight. Whenever Daniel had company, he'd wheel himself into the room and introduce himself to one and all. He had taken a particular liking to Ken's brother John—always a willing foil—and they'd even gotten their own repartee going.

"I'm Batman!" Little Billy would proclaim.

"I'm Superman!" John would answer.

Neither of them ever tired of loudly revealing his secret identity to everybody in earshot.

Little Billy also couldn't seem to get his fill of the song "Barbie Girl" by the European pop group Aqua. It had topped the dance music charts in May, and he would start bopping along to it in his wheelchair whenever he heard Ken and Nancy play it on Daniel's boom box, singing along to its chorus, "I'm a Barbie girl, in a Barbieeee world!"

"Again!" he'd shout the instant the tune was over.

Laughing, Ken and Nancy would oblige, and he'd start moving to the beat like a windup toy . . . again. And again and again and again.

But the kid's "Daniel's out of control!" line remained his show-stopper. He'd shout it out practically every time he made his entrance. Once he got his desired response, he would spin his chair around in a half circle and swing right back out the door.

This time, as usual, Ken and Nancy were an appreciative audience. Wide grins on their faces, they watched him vanish from sight as quickly as he'd appeared, then heard him yelling at the top of his lungs as he blew down the hall of the Ped wing, *"Nurse Helen, Nurse Helllllllenn . . .!"*

Halo around his head, laughter on his lips, heart filled with vibrant joy, Little Billy was one of the many kids at Rusk whom the Trushes would never forget.

CHAPTER THIRTEEN

Daniel's rehab and recovery accelerated throughout the month of August. He spoke more every day. Along with his other therapies, the tilt table—he'd officially christened those morning sessions "Tilt Table Torture Time"— had greatly increased his muscle tone and endurance. He had almost full mobility of his neck, and his upper body was stronger.

He was also regaining his appetite and putting on weight. As he started to eat more solid food, a classmate's parents placed a standing order for a neighborhood restaurant named Mumbles to deliver his favorite dish, Chicken Francaise, to his room once a week. He never got tired of it.

Daniel was still coping with serious deficits. Although he was regaining dexterity in his right hand, his left hand was partially paralyzed and would tighten with painful muscle spasms. His legs were weak, and no one could predict whether he would walk again—or how far he'd be able to go if he ever did stand up out of his wheelchair. He continued to have problems with his short-term memory, attention span, and processing of information. But he was alert, engaged, and bright eyed.

Dr. Salsberg and his staff couldn't have been happier. They knew how hard Daniel and his family had fought, but no one at Rusk had seen the boy coming so far along.

When Daniel was moved from the observation ward into his own room, his parents felt much the same as they had upon his transfer out of Beth Israel's ICU—it was a real, tangible confirmation that he'd taken a major step forward. One night their family urged them to go out to dinner, volunteering to stay with Danny until visiting hours ended. Ken and Nancy were appreciative but nervous. They hadn't had anything that resembled an evening out together since the start of Daniel's ordeal. It took considerable persuasion to finally get them to accept the offer . . . but they would be glad later on. After being in a state of siege for almost half a year, they'd needed a breather.

The family also realized Ken and Nancy would soon be under renewed stress. Daniel's medical teams at Beth Israel and Rusk had been in steady contact, and Dr. Abbott now felt he was healthy enough to return to the INN and have his aneurysms clipped.

Considered elective surgery in medical jargon, the term was misleading from a layman's perspective. The operation wasn't immediately required to save Daniel's life, but it was necessary to preserve it for the long-term. Until all five aneurysms were clipped—including the one that had burst and been coiled—Daniel was at a serious risk of another bleed. But he was only now regaining his vigor, and this would mean performing a craniotomy—opening his skull for delicate frontal lobe surgery. For his doctors the timing was a judgment call. They had to weigh their best estimation of Daniel's fitness for the surgery against waiting too long.

Ken and Nancy understood the pros and cons of going ahead with it. They'd had a number of meetings with Dr. Raul De Los Reyes, the endovascular neurologist who would lead the surgical team. He had told them there *was* a chance Daniel's remaining aneurysms would never rupture. But with one already having burst, the percentages were heightened that it would happen again. And their son would not survive a second brain hemorrhage.

If someone had been willing to enter into a pact with Ken and Nancy, and guarantee Daniel would live on exactly as he was if they decided against the surgery, neither making further progress nor getting worse, they'd have signed on the dotted line. But they didn't have that option, of course. The choice wasn't really a choice. They couldn't leave five ticking time bombs in their son's head. De Los Reyes would operate in late September.

Daniel reacted calmly—even serenely—when his parents told him about their decision. He'd been a smart kid before his injury, and his intelligence had come through intact. Dr. Rick Abbott would say it was as if he'd been reincarnated and blessed with the memory and intellect of his former life, bringing them with him to jump start a new one. Daniel understood why the operation was important, knew the risks it entailed, and tried to make the best of the situation.

Sympathetic, the doctors told Daniel he'd be permitted to return home for an extended day visit before the surgery. Since the new school year started in September, his friends all would be back in the city. Ken and Nancy planned to throw a party for him, inviting as many guests as they could squeeze into their apartment. But that was still weeks off.

Meanwhile, Michael's Uncle John and Aunt Paula had offered to take him for a drive down to Florida with his cousins Liz and

Matt. Their oldest daughter, Joanna, was down in Gainesville for the fall semester at the University of Florida, and they wanted to visit her before the start of classes. John and Paula thought it would be a fun trip for Mike that would also give Ken and Nancy a chance to mentally prepare themselves for Daniel's surgery.

Mike had a blast. He and his cousins were very close, almost like siblings. Throughout Danny's ordeal, he would spend occasional weekends in New Jersey with them, going to baseball card shows or minor league games. Now they laughed the whole ride down, playing the license plate game, trying to spot one from every state in between complaints about how long the drive was taking. Mike had early breakfasts with Nana, his aunt's mother, in Florida, often demolishing ten pancakes with whipped cream and pineapple before anyone else was awake. He spent days on end at the beach, boogie boarding and splashing in the waves. Uncle John playfully called him Fudgy the Whale.

At Rusk, Daniel had gotten well enough to participate in some of the group therapies. He loved animals, so Lisa Del Guidice introduced him to a therapy dog. Noticing the ever-present boom box in his room, Lisa arranged for him to attend music therapy sessions. Daniel would listen attentively as the therapists played different instruments and held sing-alongs with the kids, swaying to the rhythms and melodies.

With Daniel becoming more communicative by the day, Ken and Nancy enjoyed giving him the latest news about friends and relatives. He had a cork bulletin board behind his bed papered with cards, photos, and letters, and they would often read them aloud so he'd know about everyone's summer vacations. They also updated him on Mike's road trip. In Gainesville, Joanna and her boyfriend had taken him to see the alligators and turtles in Lake

Alice, on the university campus. Always the nature buff, he'd been thrilled. Before they returned to New York, his aunt and uncle capped off the excitement with a visit to the Disney theme parks, staying overnight at the Caribbean Beach Resort.

Filled with lasting memories, Mike came home at the end of August just in time to meet the baseball player John Olerud. A former all-star and winner of a pair of World Series championship rings, the first baseman was then a member of the New York Mets, whose team physicians were based at NYU and Rusk. The Mets front office would arrange for player visits to the hospital as goodwill gestures, with Lisa Del Guidice and Jill Knee, the Mets' community service director, coordinating them for Rusk's Ped unit. When Olerud agreed to meet and sign autographs for the kids, they had no clue that he'd suffered a ruptured brain aneurysm as a college student preparing to come up to the Major Leagues. The location of his injury had been almost identical to Daniel's—it was near the optic nerve—but it had leaked rather than completely burst. When he collapsed during batting practice at Washington State University, he was medevaced to the nearest hospital, where the defect was clipped before it could lead to serious complications.

Del Guidice had mentioned Olerud's visit to Ken and Nancy in advance, and they'd invited a group of Daniel's cousins and friends for the occasion. Freshly tanned from his vacation, Mike joined Daniel in hanging out and posing for snapshots with the athlete, who stayed for almost an hour. An avid baseball fan, Danny would have been overjoyed meeting a star player under any circumstances. But given what he was facing in a few short weeks, it may have been an even bigger deal to him. His family's friendship with Olerud, forged that afternoon, would be one they valued for decades to come.

The month of September arrived, the summer heat departed, and Mike started fifth grade. As Daniel's friends got back into their school and homework routines, the number of comments in his online guestbook picked up.

Ken and Nancy were quietly nervous. The day of Daniel's operation was drawing close.

───────────

On Sunday, September 21, Daniel was brought aboard an ambulette in his wheelchair and driven home, where he was met by a large welcoming party of friends and relatives.

Ken and Nancy had treasured every moment with Daniel in the weeks leading up to his operation, and they were warmed by the outpouring of affection. But their anxiety had grown with every minute that ticked by. Now the torturous countdown was almost over. As their guests filed out the door that evening, they knew Daniel's surgery was less than forty-eight hours away.

When Daniel got back to Rusk, the nurses and therapists were somber. Lisa Del Guidice became tearful. She'd seen the boy make so much progress over the past four months . . . he was a different person from when he'd first arrived. She couldn't hide her trepidation over what lay ahead.

Early Monday afternoon, Daniel and his parents were again helped into an ambulette. This time they went straight along the East River to Beth Israel.

Their return brought a flood of memories. Ken and Nancy recalled the cold night in March they were sped over with Daniel in a coma, their terror and confusion after the early diagnosis by Dr. Berenstein, and the endless nights when Daniel's intracranial pressure was soaring off the charts, rising higher than any of his doctors believed was survivable. Those were the bad memories, the anguished ones. But they also recalled the kindness of the staff, Chan Suh's gourmet food deliveries, Easter, Danny's birthday, Pepe's Tic Tac escapade, and all the many gatherings. There were good ones too.

In contrast with the mood at Rusk, the INN's staff gave Daniel a celebratory reception. They hadn't seen him since his discharge in May and were delighted by his progress. He could speak now. He made them smile. All the late nights they'd put in caring for him, all the emergency interventions, had been worth it. Ken had a sense they saw him as living proof that what they did at the INN was making a difference.

Ken and Nancy understood how the staff felt. They shared many of their emotions. But at the same time doubts and second-guesses were swirling around them like agitated wasps. What would happen to Daniel after surgery? Would he be the same as right before it? Suffer additional impairments? Or would he return to his comatose state? Would he open his eyes the first day, or would it take longer? Did he really even need the surgery at that stage, or should they have waited? If they'd waited, would another aneurysm have burst?

Ken and Nancy didn't voice any of these questions. For reasons neither could articulate, they believed they were best left unspoken. But they could see them in each other's faces.

Monday afternoon, Daniel was given a standard array of presurgical tests—blood work, X-rays, electrocardiograms. He would be restricted from eating or drinking between midnight and his surgery on Tuesday, but continued to receive nourishment through his gastronomy tube. Ken thought about sleeping over in his room but decided against it. Danny had grown accustomed to staying alone. He didn't want to alarm him by departing from that routine or doing anything else to betray his hidden worry. And he knew the boy would be in good hands at Beth Israel.

Ken and Nancy stayed with Daniel until late Monday night, waiting until the exhausted thirteen-year-old got drowsy to head home together.

The Trushes returned to the hospital early the next morning. Dr. Abbott, who'd become so heavily invested in Daniel when he was first hospitalized, met them there and told them he'd act as a sort of informal liaison with Dr. De Los Reyes, promising to keep them informed throughout the lengthy operation.

What Abbott didn't mention was that he was under no obligation to assume that role. Nor did the endovascular clipping fall within his area of expertise. But he'd sweated his blood out for Daniel in those early days. Once he'd gotten that close to a patient, gone through hell and come out the other end with him . . . he wasn't about to let Daniel backslide if he could help it.

These too weren't thoughts he shared with the boy's parents. They were private, only his to know.

That morning before surgery, Daniel was wheeled from his room into a preop room. His operation would be performed while he was under a general anesthetic, and he was given a mild sedative beforehand to relax him and lower his blood pressure. Ken and Nancy kept him company as the nurses came and went, taking his readings.

With each passing minute Ken grew quieter and more introspective. He collected his thoughts, silently asking God to give his son strength, praying everything would turn out okay. Meanwhile, Nancy talked to Daniel at his bedside, hugged him repeatedly, and fussed with his hair. The feelings of the two parents were very much alike, their ways of expressing them slightly different.

Shortly before Daniel was to be brought down to the operating room, a nurse arrived to take his blood pressure. She searched for a cuff, fumbling with several objects behind his bed.

"I guess this one will do," she said finally, thinking aloud.

Daniel couldn't see what was going on behind him and didn't know what she was referring to. But her remark was perfect comedic fodder for him.

"That doesn't sound too good," he quipped with a big smile.

Ken, Nancy, and the nurse all chuckled. His wisecrack had instantly lifted some of the tension from the room. It was hard to believe how brave and upbeat Danny was with hours of brain surgery ahead of him. He had the same aura of calm positivity that he'd shown when they'd first told him about the operation. It radiated off him, as if he had no fear over its outcome. Ken wished he could have felt as certain and free of misgivings.

Soon a group of aides and nurses showed up. Daniel was transferred from his bed to a gurney. Nancy and Ken were given permission to put on gowns and face masks and accompany Daniel into the OR, where they waited at his side until the surgical team started general anesthesia. They kissed him and held his hand. Holding back tears, trying to be strong for him, they told him they'd be right there waiting when he returned after surgery. His eyes heavy from the sedative, Daniel smiled.

Then it was time. With silent prayers, Ken and Nancy left the room.

———

With Daniel anesthetized, Dr. De Los Reyes had the nurses completely shave off the boy's hair and place his head in a metal fixation device. Then he used his surgical knife to make a curved incision in his left temple and lifted back the scalp to expose the skull. After he'd drilled several burr holes in the skull, outlining a circular bone window with them, he reached for his craniotomy saw and cut between the holes with its fine wire blade. When he'd removed the skull flap, he handed it to one of the surgical assistants, who carefully put it aside.

Reaching for a scalpel again, he sliced into the dura mater—a fibrous protective membrane around the brain—and peeled it back. Daniel's brain was now visible and accessible to De Los Reyes' through the bone window.

De Los Reyes glanced at the imaging scans, then moved the operating microscope into position and peered through its stereoscopic eyepiece, searching for the correct arterial branch. The boy's aneurysms were just as they appeared on the scans. He saw the one that had ruptured and been coiled, with the double saccular bulges his colleague, Dr. Berenstein, had called its "Mickey Mouse ears." He saw the remaining four blisters and turned his attention to the narrow areas where they sprouted off the arterial wall. He would choke them off there, at their necks, and in doing so restore the integrity of the walls across their points of weakness. It would make the blisters nonfactors. The blood pulsing through the artery would no longer have a way to fill them. Its flow would be redirected to normal vessels.

De Los Reyes would clip the aneurysms with exquisite precision. It would take patience and a light touch. They would have to be carefully pulled away from surrounding tissue and blood vessels. There was always the danger a sac would burst when it was handled. He was prepared to stop the bleeding if that occurred, but Daniel was in a vulnerable condition. De Los Reyes could see some of the scar tissue that covered the damaged parts of his brain—but only some of it. It was like looking down at a small section of a battlefield, one where unthinkable carnage had occurred not too long ago. De Los Reyes had no intention of causing more.

His eyes pressed to the microscope, he went to work.

Dr. Abbott entered Daniel's room, where his parents had been joined by family and friends who'd stopped by to lend their support.

Ken and Nancy looked at Abbott's face, saw his reassuring expression, and felt their stomachs settle. They'd been through enough with him to know when something was wrong. That wasn't the case now.

Abbott gave them his update. Daniel's aneurysms had been accessed without a problem, he said. De Los Reyes hadn't yet begun clipping them and wouldn't rush—he had a cautious, deliberate hand. But so far, so good.

Ken and Nancy thanked Abbott, told him they were appreciative of his consideration. He dismissed it as no big deal. How were they holding up? he asked. Fine, they replied.

Abbott smiled. He told them he'd check back later, nodded courteously at the others and left the room.

A moment later Ken rose off his chair, dug his fists into the small of his back, and stretched. Then he squeezed Nancy's arm and went into the small private bathroom.

Quietly shutting the door behind him, he dropped to his knees on the hard tiled floor and prayed.

Dr. De Los Reyes placed the spring-loaded clip over the aneurysm's neck with his applier, examined it closely to ascertain there were no tiny blood vessels or threads of connective tissue trapped in the clip, and released it.

The clip's jaws snapped shut around the aneurysm.

Now De Los Reyes gave the clip another look to be sure it hadn't clamped any part of the parent artery. Deciding everything was in order, he handed the clip applier to a nurse, who would sterilize it and put it back into a tray with the rest of his assortment. The tool came in a variety of configurations, some resembling pliers, tweezers, and even eyelash curlers. The shape and size of the aneurysm determined the shape and size of the applier used to insert the clip.

De Los Reyes would take one further precaution before he went on to close off the next aneurysm. Asking for a small, sharp pin, he pricked the aneurysm dome with its tip and waited. Only a small drop of blood escaped the flattened blister, confirming that no blood was flowing in from the artery. It was completely isolated.

Standing nearby, Dr. Abbott had a pleased expression on the half of his face visible above his surgical mask. As De Los Reyes had prepared to clip the aneurysm, he'd donned his scrubs and reentered the operating room "just to see what was going on."

The surgery was a long way from over. There were other aneurysms. But Abbott knew he would have more heartening news for the Trushes when he next stopped by their son's room.

Abbott kept Ken and Nancy posted all afternoon. Four hours after Daniel was brought down to the operating room, he showed up in visibly good spirits. The procedure had been concluded without any problems, he told them. De Los Reyes would soon be giving them the fuller details. But Abbott wanted them to know that all five aneurysms were clipped, and Danny was in recovery sleeping off his anesthesia. The surgery had gone so smoothly it had taken about half its estimated time.

The Trushes were elated and grateful. They promptly called their loved ones with the good word. There were still questions about how well and fast Daniel would rebound. But they were sticking by the "inch by inch" mantra.

It wasn't easy, however. When the aides wheeled him back into the ICU later that day, Ken and Nancy saw his shaved, bandaged head and immediately started putting themselves through the emotional grinder again. The procedure had been successful, yes. But had it been necessary? What had they made Daniel endure?

He barely stirred before Nancy left for home to take care of Michael. Ken stayed over at the hospital. Both would spend that pensive, sleepless night wondering if he'd show any sign of consciousness when they saw him in the morning.

It took Daniel almost a full day to wake up. To Ken and Nancy's immense relief, he was groggy but alert. He even spoke a few words, telling them he felt fine. They were overcome with admiration for him. He'd come out of brain surgery encouraging *them*.

Two or three days later, when the nurses changed his bandages, Ken gasped at the sight of the metal staples where the bone flap and covering skin had been put back into place. His head looked like a baseball. But Daniel's attitude brought both his parents greater peace about their decision to have the clipping performed. He never questioned that decision, or complained, or shed a single tear over his surgery or recuperation. Through his example of courage and acceptance, he made it all bearable for Ken and Nancy, pulled them through a forest of self-doubt, and led the way for them to eventually feel they'd done the right thing.

Daniel was discharged back to Rusk two weeks after the operation. His therapy suffered only a minor setback as he regained his strength, and he soon got back to where he was before the surgery.

His rehabilitation was going to be long. But he could now look forward to leading a full life without the menacing specter of another traumatic brain injury. Daniel was at no greater risk than anyone who'd never had a history of it. He'd kept on beating the odds.

PART THREE

THE QUIET TIME

CHAPTER FOURTEEN

February 13, 1998, landed on a Friday. The Trushes' health insurance provider had extended their benefits several times for Daniel's therapy—the caseworker's sympathetic attitude had even surprised Rusk—but now their coverage for his stay at the institute was about to expire. Daniel still had a long way to go in his rehab. His progress, though, had been nothing short of miraculous. Several weeks earlier, Nancy had seen Susan Guzzardo perform one of her most memorable feats as Warrior Princess when she'd assisted Daniel in taking his first few tentative steps out of his wheelchair—baby steps in a true sense because he was learning how to walk all over again, with a right leg that was partially paralyzed and a left that was barely strong enough to stand on. Assisting him while Nancy and her close friend Judy watched with tears in their eyes, Guzzardo had crouched and held the leg Danny couldn't move as he gripped the back of the wheelchair for support.

Daniel had only gone a few feet down the hall. Five, maybe ten. But in looking at how far he'd come since his arrival at Rusk, it might as well have been five or ten miles. Given his

family's stalwart participation in his care, his doctors and therapists believed he could successfully continue his recovery as an
outpatient.

After spending just short of a year in the hospital and rehab—
341 days—Daniel was scheduled for discharge.

Earlier in the week, the institute's head of pediatrics, Joan
Gold, had asked the Trushes if they would prefer to wait till
Saturday. She was being thoughtful. Many families would have
felt Friday the 13th an inauspicious date, and Saturday was
Valentine's Day. All flowers and flying Cupids, it had the better
reputation. Ken and Nancy had done everything Rusk's staff
could have asked of two parents, and Dr. Gold would have been
glad to postpone Daniel's release out of consideration.

The Trushes weren't superstitious. Ken didn't believe in luck,
good or bad. He believed in making the right choices, trying
your hardest, doing your best with the opportunities you were
given, and praying for God's grace to provide strength and light
your way.

He and Nancy just wanted Daniel home. For good. In
November, they'd gotten permission to bring him up to the
apartment for day trips and occasional sleepovers. They'd had to
learn how to give him medications and set up his feeding tube,
which was a little intimidating at the outset; they'd worried
about making a mistake that would cause him to have an adverse
reaction. But they soon got past their jitters and came to trea-
sure every visit as a slice of Nirvana.

Taking Daniel back to Rusk was always easier said than done.
He'd hated leaving his family, and they had hated when he left
them. The first few times, Ken and Nancy arranged to return him
in an ambulette, but after a while they switched to city buses.
The buses were more convenient; if they missed one, they could
wait for the next. With an ambulette, they had to call for their

transport in advance and be ready to go when it arrived. That seemed to shorten Danny's visits because they were constantly watching the clock as the pickup time approached.

The bus wasn't ideal either. It took a while to load Daniel aboard in his wheelchair. The driver would have to lower the ramp, leave his seat, lift up the handicapped seat to accommodate Danny's wheelchair, and then secure the safety straps to the wheelchair so it would be tethered to the floor in the event of a short stop. Ken would sometimes catch passengers giving Daniel annoyed glances. That pained him deeply, though he kept his feelings inside. After everything his son had overcome, their intolerance seemed wrong and unfair.

Those looks taught Ken something about patience, empathy, and trying to refrain from casting judgment. You never knew someone's full story. You didn't know what might be going on in a person's life, and that was true of friends as well as total strangers. Anyone could be dealing with sickness, loss, or other stressful problems. He or she didn't have to be in a wheelchair; people didn't always display their struggles and hardships in plain sight. In cities like New York, and really most places in modern society, things moved along at a frantic pace. Ken felt that only made it more important to slow down a little and be mindful of those around you.

After Daniel got home, Ken would see many more negative reactions faced by people with disabilities. They stuck with him. But the day of his son's release he was preoccupied with other things. *Old times, again,* Ken kept thinking. *Old times.* Although somehow, he knew his family would never be the same. They'd been through stratospheric highs and shattering lows, made life and death decisions, formed new relationships, solidified old ones . . . things had changed. That would be true even if Daniel returned to how he'd been before his injury.

It was as if they were a new family with a greater respect for one another, a deeper understanding of themselves as a unit. And now they were ready to help Danny reclaim as much of his life as possible.

It wasn't just Ken and Nancy who felt that way. No one could have been happier than Michael about Danny coming home. He knew he'd have to adapt. Despite his young age, he innately shared his parents' understanding that life would be different. Daniel was going to be the focus of their attention, but that wasn't the hard thing to accept. For Mike it was about what he'd lost and what he'd have to become. He had always relied on his brother to help him though all kinds of situations. Danny had been his mentor . . . his protector. That was gone now. He, Michael, would be the one with those types of responsibilities. Everything would be reversed. He'd have to be the big brother without being the big brother. He wasn't sure how to do that.

Still, when Mike awoke on the morning of February 13, he could hardly believe Danny would be back to sleeping in their room in a matter of hours.

It was unseasonably mild and spring-like for that time of year—the sun bright, the sky clear, the temperature readings in Central Park climbing to almost fifty degrees by midday. Weatherwise, it closely resembled the Sunday when Daniel had gone down in the gym . . . but that was where the similarities ended.

Ken and Nancy brought Mike along to Rusk, all three giddily piling into their Toyota station wagon for the drive downtown. They had to bottle their excitement while waiting for the discharge forms to be filled out and authorized. Finally about two o'clock in the afternoon they were ready to leave for home. Ken pulled the station wagon up to the building's exit, and they folded the wheelchair through the cargo door, putting Daniel in front where there was room for his legs and he could be more easily maneuvered.

A small family welcoming committee—Grandmas Jeanne and Eva, Grandpa Pepe, and Nancy's two sisters—was gathered at the apartment when Danny arrived half an hour later. The phone rang off the hook throughout the afternoon and evening, and all expressed their eagerness to visit. It was as if Christmas had made a smashing encore.

Daniel slept in his room from that first night on. He and Mike had trundle beds, with Mike's bed at the bottom, and their parents pulled it out further than before to allow for Daniel's feeding tube and give them a clear, unobstructed path to him in an emergency. They installed a bed guard so Daniel wouldn't roll off, and kept his wheelchair nearby in case he had to use the bathroom.

Although Daniel's overnighters had done much to prepare them for their new responsibilities, Ken and Nancy were still a little nervous about doing something wrong. They knew mistakes were inevitable and only hoped they wouldn't be serious ones when they happened. That said, they readily accepted their caregiving roles, cleaning Daniel's gastronomy tube, giving him his formula and meds, helping him get into his wheelchair every morning, helping him out of it for bathing and bedtime . . . carrying out the full range of everyday tasks his nurses and aides had performed for him at Beth Israel and later Rusk.

The Trushes were riding an emotional high, and nothing brought them down off it for weeks. About a month after Daniel's return, Ken and Nancy surprised him with a new addition to their family. Ginger the longhaired dachshund was a cute, affectionate puppy they bought at a neighborhood pet store. Daniel's fondness for the therapy dogs at Rusk had convinced Dr. Gold that he'd benefit from having his own pet, and she had encouraged his parents to get one. A dog would be a comforting presence while he was bound to a wheelchair, and Gold had hoped he'd eventually assume some of the feeding, grooming, and housebreaking duties, which would exercise his memory and accelerate his physical gains.

Daniel and Mike instantly fell for Ginger, who became their four-legged kid sister. She soon took to sitting on Daniel's lap and getting lavished with affection. Daniel loved her companionship and cuddled with her for hours on end . . . although, like most boys, he seemed perfectly content to leave the chores of caring for her to his parents.

Ken and Nancy didn't really mind. One out of two wasn't bad.

———————————

For the Trushes, Daniel's release from Rusk was a gleaming moment of triumph and promise, the start of a whole new chapter in their lives. But it was only a start. Danny still had many trials ahead of him. He had profound mobility, speech, cognitive, visual, and short-term memory issues and would need an indefinite period of outpatient therapy. The institute's daily rehab sessions commenced at nine o'clock in the morning—on the dot—a routine Danny and his parents well knew. Rusk also offered one-on-one educational support with tutors for basic math and reading skills, and Ken and Nancy were eager for their son to take advantage of the program.

With both of them working and Mike at school, the practical logistics might have been overwhelming if not for the helpfulness of their relatives. That hadn't changed at all since Daniel's early days in the hospital. Just as Ken and Nancy had formulated a visitation routine for him at Rusk, they now worked out a plan for his outpatient transport to and from the institute. But its success hinged on their leaning heavily on his grandparents and Aunt Diane.

They proved to be lifesavers. Every morning on his way to the office, Ken drove Daniel down for therapy, and every afternoon either Grandma Eva or Grandma Jeanne would pick him up and bring him home by bus. Back at the apartment, Pepe spent hours keeping his grandson company, which usually included amusing him with endless hands of blackjack. Meanwhile, Diane took charge of all the household chores she could handle. Their ready availability—their *being there*—relieved Ken and Nancy of a great deal of pressure.

Ken's appreciation for them would only grow as the weeks went by. In March or April he began to notice a drop-off in the number of calls and visits from friends. At first he was a little perplexed. He'd understood it back in the summer, when people took vacations . . . but this seemed harder to explain. While Daniel was comatose the previous spring, he'd had a constant stream of visitors at Beth Israel. Right around that time, Chan Suh had gone live with Daniel's online guestbook to give his many well-wishers a single, reliable point of contact. Now conscious and alert, Danny was becoming increasingly isolated in the apartment—and it was happening even as his parents sought to add normalcy to his routine.

Ken would never recall exactly when he made the mental link between this quiet period and the long, lonely winter after his father's burial twenty years before. But the similarity was clear once that realization set in . . . and was also comforting in its way. It was a natural transition. It didn't mean Daniel had been forgotten or that people felt differently toward him. It didn't mean they had ceased to care. They were just going about their lives. There was a point when the cheering stopped.

For Ken and the rest of his family it would be a time of continued healing and reflection, of accepting things as they were and evaluating and reassessing their goals. A time to dig deep into their hearts and minds and examine what they wanted do with their future, together and individually.

The Trushes' quiet time would last almost a decade.

Father Dennis Keane, pastor of Our Lady of Good Counsel Church, would sometimes reflect on the different ways God made Himself felt to human beings. In the Old Testament, it was through powerful, dramatic events . . . the parting of the Red Sea, or Moses' discovery of the burning bush. But in the gospels, Christ came to Simon Peter and Andrew when they were fishing. His personal Communion with His believers, and His farewell discourse, occurred during a simple meal. To Keane, it had always been significant that there were no witnesses to the Resurrection. No one saw Jesus rise. When He appeared to Mary Magdalene outside His tomb, she had thought Him a gardener.

Father Keane believed that the ordinary made extraordinary defined a key element of human faith. And today—Wednesday May 20, 1998, the day of Daniel Trush's confirmation, a celebration of a young person's growing maturity, the seal of his deepened commitment to his faith, and his reception of the Spirit of knowledge, courage, and wisdom—Keane was reflecting that the Trush family had taken some very ordinary things and made them avenues for God's presence in their lives.

Healing from an injury of the type Daniel had suffered didn't happen with a snap of the fingers, Keane thought. Nor did miracles, necessarily. Ken and Nancy constantly talking and singing to Daniel when he was comatose, their gatherings of friends and family members in his hospital room, their sharing of meals—Keane felt these ordinary things, over time and through constant process involving strong support and prayer, had contributed to the miracle of Daniel's recovery. The miracle of his *life*.

Father Keane stood looking out over the church's crowded pews. Although it was a weeknight, the nave and balcony were filled with worshippers who had arrived for Daniel's reception of the gifts of the Holy Spirit.

Our Lady of Good Counsel was a very old parish. And it was a changing parish on the East Side of Manhattan, where people came from different places, usually for career-related reasons, and stayed for four, six, seven years—they didn't live in the neighborhood long. There were people from the Philippines, Africa . . . people who were college educated, people who were bricklayers . . . but what had happened to Daniel made the entire community want to be as supportive as possible of the Trush family. It was as if they realized something unimaginably sad was being transformed into . . . Keane wasn't sure he had the words to describe it. But it was real and powerful, and it touched men and women at every level of the parish.

Father Keane had known the Trushes since he'd been assigned to Good Counsel seven years earlier . . . as he knew many families. And like many families they'd been active members of the congregation, attending music groups, and participating in different charity and fundraising drives. The two boys had been courteous and gone to services every Sunday with their parents.

They were a solid bunch. But nothing about them had seemed especially different from other families.

The day of Daniel's injury stuck out vividly in Keane's mind, though. Ken Trush had called the parish almost right away asking for his prayers, and it had occurred to Keane that not everyone would have done it so quickly. In medical emergencies of that type people called for ambulances and notified their families. They didn't always get their priest onboard. Yet somehow their family saw it as important. That prioritization didn't just spring up out of the blue, Keane had thought at the time. It had to have been there before. It showed their ingrained faith.

Father Keane had also never forgotten when he'd given Daniel the Sacrament of Anointing the Sick—his last rites. It was a couple of nights after his admission to the hospital. The boy's parents had been told he wasn't going to make it, and Keane had rushed over to see him. He remembered that, through their pain and fear, they'd had a sense of hope about them. They were going to face the terrifying thing in front of them by praying that God's will was for Daniel's health to be restored, and by hoping that they and his doctors—and Daniel himself—could accomplish what God wanted.

And, Father Keane thought, he had been restored. Above anybody's expectations.

It was a big day for Daniel and a far cry from the days and nights when he'd lain in coma, no one knowing how many more had been left to him.

Nancy's sister Diane, who had left the medal of Saint Padre Pio of Pietrelcina under Daniel's pillow at Beth Israel, was his sponsor, the person given the honor of accompanying him to the altar. Daniel wanted to walk up the church's aisle rather than receive the sacraments in his wheelchair, and that had worried his parents—he'd barely taken any steps out of the chair, none of them without assistance. But for a day as significant and memorable as his confirmation, with so many friends and family members invited to the ceremony, Ken and Nancy felt their son deserved to make the call. And he'd chosen to stand on his feet.

When the time came, Daniel rose out of his chair with Nancy and Diane on either side of him, the two all but holding him upright. Slowly, haltingly, they made their way down the aisle to a waiting Father Keane.

The clapping broke out well before the little group reached the chancel. It came pouring down from the balcony overhead and rose from pews running back toward the doors, spreading from aisle to aisle. By the time Daniel reached the front of the altar, the loud waves of applause had filled the entire church.

Looking at the young man's crying mother and aunt through emotional tears of his own, Father Keane had to wait a while for the clapping to die down before he began his homily.

CHAPTER FIFTEEN

Ken did a lot of running in the summer of '98. Basketball had been his first passion, and he'd always done sprints and intervals to stay in shape for the game. But as he'd gotten older, his chronic soreness, knee surgery, and a slew of minor injuries on the court convinced him to give it up. Seeking a different athletic outlet, he took up long-distance running.

In the beginning it felt like slow, boring torture. However, as Ken's lungs and legs adjusted to its rigors, he came to find the activity very peaceful. Although it offered no substitute for the competitive rush of basketball, he embraced it as a close second.

The year Daniel was injured, Ken had been running diligently four times a week. He wasn't all that fast, but it kept his body fit and suited his goal-setting predispositions. His longest runs were reserved for Sundays in Central Park, after he'd stretched, prayed, and given thanks. He was invigorated by the scenery, the fresh air, and the breeze coming over the Reservoir with its mingled scents of water, earth, and foliage. The steady rhythms of his feet touching the ground and his regular, controlled breathing calmed and leveled him.

Ken had run when Daniel was at Beth Israel, and he'd run throughout his son's nine months at Rusk. It had helped to clear his mind, shake off stress, and restore his inner balance. He'd repeatedly seen many of the same runners in the park and gotten friendly with them. Their conversations had been temporary reprieves from the long ordeal playing out for his family in one hospital room after another.

That summer Ken had been concerned about Daniel's psychological and emotional health. In the five months since his discharge, Danny's life had been pared down to a strenuous program of outpatient therapy at the institute and home workouts. He still couldn't walk without assistance and needed to be held under each arm just to go a few short feet from his wheelchair. Often he had to be half-carried, half-dragged along, his weight supported by whoever was helping him. But he'd doggedly kept at it.

Ken could not have taken greater pride in his son. He admired his courage, tenacity, and the way he went about his rehab without objection or complaint. But his socializing was mostly limited to his family. In June, Ken and Nancy had transferred his therapy to Beth Israel because it was closer to where they lived than Rusk. But the hospital didn't offer tutoring and they'd arranged for Daniel to receive home instruction, adding to the amount of time he spent in the apartment. He had few things to break the deadly tedium.

Ken had wondered if there might be activities that would give Danny a chance to get out and mingle with people. Things they might be able to do together. Ken was no expert, but he figured fresh air and exercise would bring more oxygen to his son's brain and bloodstream. That seemed a good, commonsense formula, anyway.

He started asking different runners whether they knew of anything, and somebody advised him to call the New York Road Runners Club, who suggested he call the Achilles Track Club. He'd never heard of it before, but what he learned would ignite his enthusiastic interest.

Founded by Dr. Dick Traum in 1983, Achilles was a running, rolling, and walking organization for people with disabilities. Then in his late fifties, Traum had gotten one leg amputated after a car accident that occurred when he was a grad student. Years later he'd started running at a local YMCA to get in shape and wound up training for different races. At the time very few amputees were competing, and the sight of Traum on his prosthetic leg had raised many surprised eyebrows.

He'd continued to surprise almost everyone when he became the first amputee to run the New York City Marathon, completing it in just short of seven and a half hours. This was in 1976; a few years later he founded the Achilles Track Club.

Achilles matched disabled runners with able-bodied volunteers, who worked with them to achieve specific personal goals or train for large mainstream events. When Ken phoned the club for information, he was told about two separate programs: the adult training program and Achilles Kids for disabled children and young adults. Now fourteen, Daniel was old enough to meet the age requirements for either category, so Ken decided to investigate both and see which was the better fit.

The Achilles adults met Tuesday evenings and Saturday mornings at the 90th Street and Fifth Avenue entrance to Central Park. One Saturday in July, Ken put on his sweatpants and sneakers, helped Daniel into his wheelchair, and rolled him a few blocks to the park from their apartment building. When they got there the place was crowded with disabled walkers and runners. Coordinators were pairing them up with volunteer coaches and organizing them into groups. The mood was lively and filled with camaraderie. Everybody went out of the way to make Ken and Danny feel welcome and part of things.

That first day flew by. Although he barely left his wheelchair, Danny had a magnificent time meeting people who were also facing challenges and could relate to his situation. When Ken saw the happiness on his face as they went walking through the park, he knew they *belonged*.

After that Ken and Daniel started going to the Achilles meets every Saturday morning. Most days, Mike went with them. Exercising and socializing with other Achilles runners gave Danny a break from his otherwise regimented outpatient schedule. Nadine McNeil, whose young son Tyler was autistic, and Artie Elefant, a runner and cyclist who was losing his vision due to a degenerative eye condition, became frequent companions. Dave Wolf had been a high school track star when he suffered a traumatic brain injury. Though Wolf was almost twenty years older than Daniel, they hit it off at once. The two were kindred spirits, their indefatigable, no-boundaries attitudes and offbeat senses of humor closely in synch. Daniel and Wolf would sing the theme song from the old TV sitcom *The Brady Bunch*—a tradition Danny and his roommates at Rusk had started as they filed off to start their morning rehab—once Danny could talk, that was—and howl with laughter as they belted it out. They soon became regular walking buddies, kidding around endlessly as they pushed each other on.

For Ken the beauty of Achilles was that Daniel could set individualized benchmarks and work toward them at his chosen pace. Nothing was imposed on him. That freedom just inspired him to work harder. Even when Danny's coaches integrated therapeutic exercises into his walks, they did their best to make them fun. They would walk backwards and sideways while flapping their arms like wings and, helping Daniel out of his wheelchair, ask him to follow suit. They'd call sudden halts without warning, everyone stopping on a dime, and Danny would try to do the same. They knew they were an oddball sight and got a kick out of it. The bigger the spectacle they made of themselves, the more they laughed.

Danny also loved Achilles Kids. Led by Karen Lewis, who was herself an athlete with disabilities, it wasn't nearly as goal-oriented as the adult program but instead provided exercise to challenged youngsters in an entertaining format. Karen was always ready with hugs and encouragement, and tried to make her events memorable for the children. Danny made many friends his age at the Kids races, minimarathons, and other events.

Between his therapy at Rusk and the Achilles Saturdays, Daniel's routine had gotten busy and varied. His Achilles Saturdays helped strengthen his mind and body, enriching his life in ways his father had never envisioned when he'd phoned the Road Runners Club with his initial inquiry.

The experience was no less transformative for Ken and Nancy. To them it underscored the difference an accepting environment could make for individuals who'd been sidelined or ostracized because of their disabilities. People were essentially social beings. But the disabled spent much of their time in isolation or engaged one-on-one with therapists. That increased their feelings of apartness. Socialization and acceptance did the opposite, giving them confidence, building their self-esteem, conquering fear and rejection. Ultimately it brought about a sense of community. There was magic in bringing people together, the wonderful power to change lives. Through kindness toward one another, collaborative effort, and union, they could come to share a precious gift: the strength to endure it all.

Ken and Nancy would often think—and talk—about that in years to come, as Daniel slowly continued his recovery.

———————

The Trushes spent much of August preparing for September.

Throughout the summer, Daniel had heard some of the Achilles runners discussing the Fifth Avenue Mile, a late-September road race that spanned twenty blocks along Manhattan's historic thoroughfare. By mid-August he and Ken had decided to participate.

Daniel's body wasn't quite ready for the mile. But he'd built up his strength, stamina, and coordination and had been walking longer and farther without assistance. The same inner drive he'd tapped to wring the most out of his endless painful hours on the tilt table made him want to compete. It wasn't about comparing his ability to anyone else's; it was about setting a bar for himself and doing his best to achieve it.

Meanwhile, Ken and Nancy had begun to look ahead toward Daniel's upcoming school year. Before his discharge from Rusk, David Salsberg and Jennifer Freiman Bender had given Daniel a clinical smorgasbord of intelligence and achievement tests with names like WISC-III, WRAT-III, GORT-IV, and the California Verbal Learning Test. Their description of his performance was broken down into functional strengths and weaknesses. As Daniel's strengths, they listed "General fund of knowledge and information, social knowledge, and comprehensive vocabulary." His weaknesses were enumerated as "Difficulty accessing knowledge base. Visual, perceptual and motor skills. Visual alertness to missing details. Social judgment. Visual sequencing. Ability to make familiar objects from puzzle pieces—visual memory."

Daniel's abstract reasoning and mathematical skills—he took great pride in the latter—also might have been placed in the "strengths" column. On the whole, Daniel's assessments indicated that his mental hard drive was full of learned information but that his injury had compromised his ability to access and use the data. His biggest difficulty was in "information processing speed" due to his memory difficulties. He'd sometimes need short cues to help him access the information that was there but perhaps had been stored in parts of the brain with damaged pathways leading to them. Encouragingly, his later scores showed consistent gains in all areas.

Soon after Daniel came home in February, Ken and Nancy were asked to bring him into a conference with a CSE, or Committee on Special Education, consisting of psychologists, educators, and parent advocates from the New York City Board of Education. The meeting was straightforward. Based on their reading of Salsberg's tests and other evaluations, the CSE's finding was that the mainstream school system couldn't offer Daniel the "extensive individualized support" he needed. Its recommendation was that Ken and Nancy arrange for him to have one-on-one home instruction while continuing his outpatient therapies at Rusk.

Daniel started his home schooling in May and did well, working hard to continue his improvements. But when Ken and Nancy saw how positively he'd responded to his Saturday Achilles walks—and to hanging out with his new friends at the breakfasts and informal gatherings Ken often pulled together—they felt it was time for him to transition into a classroom environment and be around other kids his age.

There were hurdles, however. First, Daniel would still need special education services, and that meant getting him into the right program. But how? *Was* there such a program? If so, where? Ken and Nancy were on uncharted ground again.

It was a neuropsychologist and rehabilitation counselor named Dr. Tamar Martin who would assist them in finding answers. With her city-bred, no-nonsense approach, Martin combined a natural warmth and compassion with toughness, savvy, and a piercing, attentive intelligence. Her dark-brown eyes were keen and focused, and you knew she was taking your measure when she met you. These qualities ideally suited her role as lead psychologist for the Traumatic Brain Injury—Technical Assistance Project at Mount Sinai Medical Center.

Martin was a friend of Danny's homeschool teacher and, in fact, had recommended her to the Trushes early on. When Ken and Nancy mentioned they wanted Danny's schooling to go in a new direction, she immediately thought of a special program for students with TBI run by the Southern Westchester BOCES, or Boards of Cooperative Educational Services.

In 1948, the New York state legislature had created BOCES to provide shared educational services to its sparsely populated rural districts. BOCES was offered in Westchester, Long Island, and throughout the rest of the state, but the five boroughs of New York City and other urban areas were excluded from membership because they theoretically had the tax-based resources to pay for those services.

But the city's economic makeup had changed since the forties, and its public school system had no equivalent to the Westchester County TBI program, which integrated academic classes and therapy for a small number of students in a school setting. Martin had been visiting Daniel for weekly remediation to help with his memory and basic academic skills, and she felt the BOCES program would be a perfect alternative to his home instruction.

Ken and Nancy weren't sure. They agreed that its curriculum offered exactly what they'd wanted. But the commute out to Westchester was almost an hour each way. Daniel would have to wake up no later than six o'clock every morning for the six-thirty school bus. He'd have a long schedule of classes and therapy until three in the afternoon, then get home around four o'clock looking at hours of homework. Danny had been doing remarkably well, but he wasn't close to being at full strength. After his nine arduous months at Rusk, Ken and Nancy hesitated to submit him to that punishing daily routine.

A drive out to meet the BOCES team at Martin's urging eased their concerns, however. The instructors and therapists seemed friendly, understanding, and thoroughly acquainted with the needs of TBI students. Their compassion and professionalism convinced Ken and Nancy to give it a shot.

Martin was glad. But she realized there might yet be impediments to Danny's placement. The New York City public school system was responsible for providing special education services for school-age children within the five boroughs. While Daniel's eligibility wasn't an issue, the cost of those services might be, since the city legally had to pay for them. Ken and Nancy would again have to meet with a Board of Education committee. With Martin and their appointed advocate present, they would have to make a case that the BOCES program was the most appropriate one for Daniel and win the committee's go-ahead.

Martin began writing up her referral. She'd been through these hearings before. The Board of Education characterized itself as a partner with the parents and family members of special-needs kids. But when it came down to footing the bill, she knew things could get rough.

Although Daniel's physical limitations ruled out rigorous training for the Fifth Avenue Mile, he'd been doing his best to prepare for it in the latter days of summer. He would walk a block holding onto his wheelchair and go another block with Ken pushing him in the chair, alternating as they strolled from their apartment to Central Park. When they reached the park, they would follow a similar routine using lamp poles as distance markers, counting the number of poles Danny passed while walking before he grew fatigued. Each Saturday morning they would try to top the previous week's record.

By August, Ken estimated that Daniel would be able to walk a quarter to a half mile holding onto his wheelchair. His right leg dragged, and he needed at least one person at his side to occasionally steady him. But he could go that far.

For Daniel it wasn't far enough. The race wasn't called the Fifth Avenue *Quarter to Half* Mile. When he and his father had decided to try it, he'd been all in from start to finish. Now they could concede part of the distance or find a strategy for walking it.

Neither Ken nor Daniel saw the first as a real choice.

Ken and Nancy's appearance with Daniel before the reconvened Committee for Special Education was a tense affair. Dr. Martin had advised them that the school board might take a critical view of her recommendation that Daniel attend BOCES classes. She'd thought they might be adamant that he continue using the services available within his local school district.

Martin would accompany the Trushes to the session. She was prepared to argue on Daniel's behalf that the district had no special programs for students with TBI. She intended to stress that his glowing school reports before his injury, his extraordinary efforts to recover from it, and his friendly, upbeat personality made him an excellent candidate for the mainstreaming opportunities BOCES offered its students. She also had written documentation of his steady progress under therapy and home instruction.

Going into the session, Martin reminded Ken and Nancy to emphasize their family's stability, community standing, and commitment to Daniel's education. Most of all, she reminded them to be themselves.

They sat down at the large, rectangular conference table feeling nervous but prepared. A major decision about their son's future rested in the hands of the committee. But things had worked for him before. Ken and Nancy tried to stay confident they would again.

Two hours after the meeting began, Tamar Martin exited the conference room feeling like she was ten feet off the ground. She'd been pleasantly caught off guard by the amiable tone of the board's questions, their reaction to the Trushes' answers— and most of all by their preliminary determination. Speaking in general terms, they'd agreed to a member that Daniel was perfectly suited for BOCES. Although Ken and Nancy still had to await their specific recommendations, Martin told them she'd never been in a CSE meeting that had gone as well.

As the Trushes were about to head home, they got another surprise: One of the Board of Ed representatives discreetly asked them to step into his office. Closing the door behind them, he said, "Daniel should receive all services he needs. We shouldn't allow any deviation from that. If it happens, you fight it."

Ken and Nancy thanked him and left, stunned. When they'd first brought Daniel into the conference room, they hadn't known exactly what they would find inside. But the last thing they'd expected was a room full of advocates.

Ken pushed Daniel's wheelchair from the elevator into the lobby of their apartment building, exchanged good-morning greetings with the man at the security desk, and then rolled Daniel outside. It was a little before 6:30 AM on a mid-September weekday, and even at that early hour the weather was on the warm side. Autumn was in no hurry to arrive; the long range forecast called for balmy temperatures through the last Sunday of the month, when the Fifth Avenue Mile would take place. For Daniel a slight cooling would be ideal. He burned a lot of calories willing himself to do simple physical activities most people took for granted, and tended to quickly work up a sweat with prolonged exertion.

Looking across the courtyard and to his left, Ken saw the yellow charter school bus waiting near the curb cut at the intersection. He pushed Danny out of the court to the sidewalk and walked toward the bus.

The driver and school bus matron lowered the ramp for Danny's wheelchair and then came around to help him onboard. Ken lingered on the sidewalk for several moments after the bus pulled away, watching it go east toward the highway and Willis Avenue Bridge en route to Westchester. It occurred to him that he felt like the typical working parent, putting his child on a school bus. He hadn't had that feeling for many months. Not remotely.

Finally Ken turned toward the parking garage where he kept his car, and headed off to the office. When Daniel returned at four o'clock, he would be met by Nancy, Grandma Eva, or his Aunt Diane. With his therapy integrated into the BOCES school's routine, he didn't have to make any more trips to the hospital for outpatient rehab. Instead he'd do his homework, Nancy helping him with his English and science assignments, and later on Ken with his math. Michael, meanwhile, had already begun spending a little more time with his school friends . . . another sign of greater normalcy. For the past year and a half, the bulk of Mike's after-school hours had been spent in medical facilities.

Thinking about all this as he drove downtown, Ken was reminded, and not for the first time, that Daniel wasn't the only member of his family moving forward on the road to recovery.

———————

The temperature on the day of the Fifth Avenue Mile rose into the eighties. Spectators in shorts and T-shirts lined up behind the barricades along the race's ruler-straight route, which went from 80th Street to 60th Street on the eastern margin of Central Park.

Flanked by his parents, Mike, and an Achilles volunteer named Laura, Daniel would undertake the race in a white T-shirt and loose-fitting black sweat pants that fit comfortably over his leg brace. He would have his wheelchair as backup in case he fatigued . . . but that never happened despite the warm, humid weather.

Danny had decided to concentrate on distance instead of time for his first race. The plan was for him to walk a few blocks, then sit in his chair to rest for a few minutes, then walk again. When he paused to rest in the chair, it was just that. A pause and a quick sip of water. He refused to be pushed an inch. If he went the mile, he would do it walking.

It took Daniel forty-five minutes to complete the mile, Ken to his right, Laura to his left, Nancy pushing the wheelchair as Mike walked slightly apart from them holding a water bottle, his eyes squared on Danny. As he approached the arching white banner with the word FINISH printed in the middle, a smile appeared on Daniel's face, growing larger and larger with each step that brought him closer to it. But it was only when his foot touched the painted line, and not an instant sooner, that Danny proudly raised his hands in the air, using the right hand to straighten his tight left arm and pull it up over his head . . . pull it up high, high, as high as he could get it to reach.

"I did it," he exclaimed. *"I did it!"*

Ken, Nancy and Mike just stood there smiling quietly, watching him bask in the crowd's heartfelt cheers and applause.

CHAPTER SIXTEEN

Daniel attended BOCES from the autumn of 1998 through June 2000, taking large strides forward over the course of two full years.

The Traumatic Brain Injury program was in a separate building on the grounds of Horace Greeley High School in southern Westchester County. The students would have a group class and individual therapies in that facility and then break off and mainstream in certain subjects with the high school. Assigned a special-needs aide, Daniel took earth science, math, and health education as a mainstream student.

Greeley's student population shared its cafeteria with TBI students, and Daniel enjoyed having lunch—and occasionally a donut or egg sandwich breakfast—with the mainstream kids, who were for the most part accepting and friendly toward him. His outgoing nature made him popular among both student bodies. Besides attending to his studies and therapy, he was doing what outgoing fourteen-year-olds did in school environments— having fun with classmates, making friends . . . and developing crushes. He had a crush on Kathy, but she was Joseph's girl-friend. Meanwhile, Alyssa, a girl in Daniel's BOCES class, only had eyes for him.

In his special education curriculum Daniel was encouraged to keep journal entries about what he did during his weekends and then share his experiences with his fellow students. He was also required to discuss current events stories with the class. The journal was a good timeline-building vehicle intended to aid his recall and verbal performance. The news discussions likewise flexed his communication skills and offered multiple benefits for his ability to retrieve, retain, and analyze information.

The approach Daniel's teachers used to address his short-term memory difficulties generally revolved around patience, repetition, and structure. "Although his attention span is quite good, his processing speed is slow," wrote Tamar Martin. "Thus, he performs best when provided with additional time to complete assignments." Dr. Martin's recommended teaching strategies for him were nutshelled by a single sentence on her list: "Try not to rush Daniel."

Her evaluation neatly meshed with Ken Trush's adopted inch-by-inch mantra. He and Daniel had unfalteringly stuck to its practice, with growing emphasis on Danny's training for distance races. After the '98 Fifth Avenue Mile, he'd started to walk regularly with his friend from Achilles, Dave Wolf, the two of them training to lower his mile times and compete in longer 5k—five-kilometer—races. But the Fifth Avenue Mile remained Daniel's benchmark for his progress, and each year's edition of the race became a September highlight. In 1999, Daniel halved his original time to twenty minutes. He was pleased but not close to satisfied. He intended to shave at least another minute off his pace the following year.

Above and beyond anything else, the Trush family delighted in the typical things parents and their kids did together. Ken would bring the boys to ball games while Nancy often took them to the Central Park zoo and museums, where they'd see polar bears, sea creatures, dinosaur fossils, ancient artifacts and mummies. Each visit was a new journey of discovery. Sometimes the whole family piled into the family car for weekend jaunts outside the city and trips to a drive-though safari in New Jersey, where Ken and the boys would reliably get a kick out of Nancy's joyful feeding of the animals—she couldn't resist when begging giraffes and baboons stuck their heads and hands through the wagon's open window. Their family felt liberated from the ordered sameness of days, weeks, and months in hospital rooms. They felt grateful to have Daniel back after having almost lost him forever on so many occasions. They felt they'd received a miracle and were appreciative of it.

Still, Ken and Nancy worried about Daniel's feeling lonely, bored, and alienated, especially during the summer months. For most young teens, getting into the swing of summer meant long hours swimming, hiking, camping, playing pickup basketball and baseball games, or just hanging out with other kids their age. It meant putting on a pair of shorts, lacing up your sneakers, and heading out into days filled with infinite possibility. But there was no escaping the reality that Daniel couldn't take part in many of the activities boys loved. Some of the doors that were open to them weren't available to him. He was largely excluded from the unexplored heaven that stretched between one school year and the next.

Aware of this, his parents sought ways to keep him busy and engaged, and with the assistance of Daniel's teachers and therapists, they found other doors for him. During the summer of '99, Daniel went to a BOCES summer camp for a few weeks; the following year he would attend Mount Sinai Hospital's free

Phase II program for individuals with brain injury, which had fun, stimulating group sessions that helped with his cognitive recovery.

Life went on for the Trushes and, like any family, they had their ups and downs. The spring of 2000 brought a period of unforeseen transition, beginning with a painful new discovery and test of their resilience: Nancy's mother Eva was diagnosed with advanced colon cancer in May. Ken was in the room when her doctors had to abort the colonoscopy because the tumor was so large it blocked the probe from entering her intestine. Eva's physicians weren't optimistic about her prospects.

Around the same time, BOCES informed Ken and Nancy that the TBI program would be moving to a location further north from Manhattan for the fall semester and that its curriculum would be shifting from an academic to an exclusively vocational model. Ken and Nancy discussed their options and agreed they wanted Daniel to continue on an academic track. But where would he go? Caught by surprise, they had to evaluate their options for Daniel's education even as they tried to absorb the dire news about Eva.

In June, Ken spoke to Chan Suh about taking an indefinite leave from Agency. Before Daniel's injury, he'd often gone in to the office seven days a week. After March '98, Ken had shuttled constantly between Agency, Beth Israel, and Rusk. When the company went public in '99, it had meant nonstop action for him as its executive vice president.

The schedule had taken a toll. Ken wanted to spend more time with his family, and he wanted Nancy to spend as much time as she desired with her critically ill mother. If he stayed home with the boys, that would make it possible. He also felt it would allow him to do more for Danny and Mike's mental, spiritual, and physical advancement.

Ken said good-bye to Agency on the last day of June. With Eva slated for extensive surgery and Mike and Daniel starting their summer vacations, his role as stay-at-home dad immediately became a busy one. Meanwhile, he and Nancy had to find a suitable new school for Danny.

Their hunt wasn't all that dissimilar from the experience they'd had looking for a rehab facility before Danny's discharge from Beth Israel. They visited several special-needs schools in the city and another out on Long Island. But it was one dead end after another. Most of the schools were geared toward students who were exclusively learning disabled, and Daniel had physical disabilities to consider. Although he'd gone a long way toward freeing himself from his wheelchair, he still needed to use it, especially when he was tired or fatigued. Ken and Nancy were surprised to discover that some of the schools weren't even wheelchair accessible.

Finally a family friend recommended The Smith School, a small alternative school located in the basement of a neighborhood church. Founded in 1990, it offered a personalized curriculum to children that its director, Karen Smith, termed "fragile" students—kids who would face a variety of obstacles in traditional academic environments. After his evaluation, Daniel was invited to visit the school for an all-day trial session. It went well, and he was accepted for the fall semester.

Meanwhile, Nancy's mother had been slated for surgery. Her doctors refused to make predictions about her long-term survival but said they would have to be aggressive in the operating room to give her a chance. Near the end of June, they removed the malignant growth and a portion of her colon. Eva would now face months of radiation and chemo.

With Ken pitching in at home, and Mike away at camp, Nancy was able to spend much of the summer helping Pepe and her sisters with her mother's care. When Daniel wasn't occupied with Phase II and training for his third Fifth Avenue Mile, Ken would take him—and Mike after he returned from sleepaway camp—to ball games, museums, and other places fathers and sons typically went together. Anytime they could manage it, the whole family packed into the car for their weekend adventures. Daniel would light up during those day trips. They were total departures from the structured routines with which he was so familiar.

When Ken saw how much he enjoyed those outings, he decided to try to keep some of their loose, easy spontaneity in Daniel's life after he started school. Since Daniel only had half days on Fridays, with classes ending at noon, Ken reasoned that he could pick him up and drive to a surprise destination every week. It would be a day when anything could happen—one Danny could look forward to. All he'd know in advance was that he was going someplace special. Ken understood it wouldn't entirely substitute for him being with friends his age. But it would be another open door.

So, in September, Fun Fridays kicked off. The mystery attraction might be a bowling alley or miniature golf course, Yankee Stadium, Madison Square Garden, Rockefeller Center, or a tour of Radio City Music Hall. They would go to movies and street fairs, visit the Statue of Liberty and Ellis Island, and have lunch at themed restaurants.

True to form, they had a running routine when they got in the car.

"Where are you taking me?" Daniel would ask.

"If I told ya, I'd have to kill ya," Ken would respond, doing his best movie gangster impression.

They always laughed at that together as he pulled into traffic.

———————————

With their ongoing focus on Daniel's recovery and Eva's post-operative treatments, Ken and Nancy recognized Michael might be feeling deprived of attention. It just seemed there weren't enough hours in the day to do everything that had to be done. They hoped Mike realized how much they loved him, but it was hard to tell. He stayed quiet about his thoughts and always assured them he was okay. But he'd lost a lot of his childhood to the past three years. They worried he felt forgotten.

Ken and Nancy tried their hardest to give him a sense of inclusion and importance. When they couldn't plan family activities, they'd do things separately with him.

Ken balanced Daniel's Fun Fridays with Michael's Early Saturday Mornings with Dad. It didn't sound as catchy but Ken took equal pleasure in those times. Mike was an early riser—hence Ken's designation for the outings—and the two would leave the apartment between 6:30 and 7:00 AM. Customarily they'd walk to a nearby health food store, where Ken would pick up a granola wrap and then head on over to Burger King so Mike could savor one of the breakfast combos. That was the set part of the morning; the rest would be strictly improvised. They might run a lap around the Central Park Reservoir or go hiking in Jersey's Greenbrook nature sanctuary. They might shag balls in the little park outside their building, hit the batting cages at Randall's Island in the East River, or drive over to Shea Stadium in Queens to try to get player autographs before catching a game. Every so often they'd go fishing for fluke on a party boat out of Captree State Park. Once Mike caught the largest fish and won the whole betting pool. It gave all the experienced fishermen on the boat a kick.

As Mike got older and baseball captured more of his interest, Ken would take him for batting lessons with a coach on Long Island on Wednesday evenings. It was an hour's car ride in each direction, and they would chat the whole way back and forth, playing Mike's favorite hip-hop songs on the stereo. Ken would relish those drives for the opportunity they gave them to talk and bond—and for the chance he got to bone up on the latest musical trends as Mike rapped along with Jay-Z.

Throughout their times together, he was astonished by how at ease Mike was with himself; he possessed a maturity and contentment that went far beyond his years. Ken wondered then, and later, whether these qualities, and his selfless, giving spirit, were innate in him or had developed out of the events surrounding Daniel's injury. Maybe it was a combination of both. And in the end, it wasn't all that important.

For his parents, the main thing was just to appreciate the person he was.

The elite runner who won the 2000 Fifth Avenue Mile finished in a few ticks over four minutes. Once again using his wheelchair for backup, Daniel cut his time to nineteen minutes—down a full minute from the previous year. He didn't win any medals, but everyone there to root for him knew he was a champion.

Danny celebrated the moment and then put it behind him. He'd met his goal and was happy about it. But he was determined to bring his pace down even more in 2001.

CHAPTER SEVENTEEN

In June 2003, Daniel received his special high school diploma from The Smith School, only one year after he'd have graduated from Dalton. He was now nineteen years old.

It was a time of great joy for Ken and Nancy. It was also a daunting, frightening time. The feelings were contradictory yet inseparable.

As Danny's final semester had drawn to an end, and he had met the requirements for graduation, Ken and Nancy had begun pondering the directions his life might take—and what paths were available to him. That had been very clear cut when September denoted the start of another school year. But now he'd be out of school . . . or would he? The Individuals with Disabilities Education Act of 1990 mandated that states provide an appropriate education program for every special needs student until his or her twenty-first birthday. Daniel's case had been subject to regular Board of Education reviews, and his consistent progress at The Smith School guaranteed he'd be eligible to take courses there for another two years, with the Trushes likely getting reimbursed for the bulk of his tuition.

Many people had advised Ken and Nancy to take full advantage of the IDEA provisions and keep him at Smith longer. But they felt Danny had gained everything possible from high school level courses, and that it would only postpone his future. He'd earned his diploma and felt ready to move on.

But move on where? To what? His parents were concerned about all the uncertainty ahead of Daniel. Ken, in particular, couldn't stop thinking about it. Nancy always had been better suited to accepting and appreciating things as they were. Ken's mindset was different. He looked at objectives, targets, concrete strategies. He and Nancy both wanted Daniel to feel valued, successful and fulfilled. But how would he achieve these things? What direction would he take? Was an advanced education an option? *What to do?*

Daniel's commencement was marked by a small, beautiful ceremony on Manhattan's East Side. The graduating class had less than ten students, and the guests were limited to Daniel's parents, Mike, and their close family members: Daniel's Aunts Diane, Paula and Debbie, his Uncles John and Steve, his grandparents Jeanne, Pepe and, to everyone's delight, Grandma Eva. Three years after her cancer diagnosis, Nancy's mother was a survivor. She'd rebounded from the surgery, chemotherapy, and radiation to see Danny receive his diploma.

His parents beamed with pride as they watched the ceremony, putting their worries about Daniel's future on hold. But the matter would preoccupy them throughout the summer. The *what to do?* question haunted Ken, who'd gone back to Agency on a part-time basis when the company had some major decisions to consider. At home with Daniel while she was on vacation, Nancy found her mind drawn to the question as well.

Together, Ken and Nancy did their utmost to seek out answers. In July they secured volunteer positions for Daniel at the Rusk

Institute and Beth Israel, but the Rusk job—assisting Lisa Del
Guidice with the kids in the playroom—was only for two hours
a week, and Beth Israel was strictly on Tuesdays, leaving Danny
with a lot of free time.

He loved helping out at both places, though. The children at
once viewed him as an adult authority figure and related to his
disabilities. At Rusk, Del Guidice soon discovered it made him
a kind of role model to them. In the kids' eyes, he was *one* of
them. Taller, older, but one of them. Some of the more reserved
children would be quick to overcome their shyness or mistrust
when Del Guidice paired them up with him.

"Hi, I'm Danny, what's your name?" he'd say with a smile when
he introduced himself. His open, genuine personality usually
won them over right off.

When Daniel laughed at the visiting clown's hokey antics,
they felt it was okay to laugh too. When he picked up a coloring
book, they would gravitate to him with their crayons. Del
Guidice enjoyed watching him interact with them. Daniel's
enthusiasm made everything fun, and the occasional struggles
he faced because of his short-term memory problems only
endeared him more to the children. If he lost track of a move
while playing a board game, he'd stick with it, leading with his
heart. The kids invariably followed that lead, sometimes even
nudging his recollection.

Meanwhile, Ken and Nancy kept seeking a path for Daniel,
a way for him to follow his passions and do something meaningful. They investigated additional volunteering opportunities, but when the interviewers heard he had TBI and mobility
issues, they'd be politely dismissed. Frustrated, they researched
Daily Habilitation facilities. The Day Habs, as they were
called, offered to help adults with cognitive challenges achieve

greater personal independence and better employment skills. But thanks to Rusk, BOCES, The Smith School, and his own determination, Daniel's abilities were already far in advance of what their programs offered—and he felt he had it within himself to go further. The Day Habs weren't for him.

A meeting with a TBI counselor left Ken and Nancy discouraged. She simply recommended they provide Daniel with a daily caregiver, which seemed less a plan for his future than a supplement to a plan. What was Daniel going to do with his life while under a caregiver's assistance? The counselor had no answers.

Ken and Nancy continued their search. Their optimism got a boost midway through the summer when they heard about a government agency called Vocational and Educational Services for Individuals with Disabilities, or VESID. The agency's stated purpose was, in part, to give "access to a full range of employment and independent living services that may be needed by persons with disabilities throughout their lives." It emphasized that it was "designed to focus on our customers and produce results."

With a fair amount of anticipation, Ken and Nancy made an appointment for Daniel to see a vocational specialist at VESID's district office in midtown. The personalized aspect of the agency's mission statement seemed right in line with their goals.

The Trushes had all looked forward to the consultation, and two hours in the waiting room did nothing to blunt their eagerness. But when they were called into the specialist's office, she rushed through their meeting in under ten minutes, asking a handful of basic questions about Daniel and his disability.

Her recommendation was a dishwashing job. The Trushes were staggered. How could she make that suggestion after barely speaking to him? They recognized that Daniel had limitations. But as a thirteen-year-old he'd overcome every obstacle to his survival. He'd relearned how to speak, read, write, and move his limbs. He'd walked when no one thought he would ever leave his wheelchair. There was no shame in being a dishwasher. But at nineteen, wasn't he entitled to aspire? Hadn't he earned an assessment based on his accomplishments rather than his disabilities? Didn't everyone deserve that much?

What to do, what to do?

Ken and Nancy were at their wits' end. They were running out of summer, up against the calendar, and Daniel was still adrift, without a plan. Doubt slid into their thoughts. They felt a pressure born of weeks of anxiety, frustration and disappointment. Should they have listened to the people who'd advised them to keep Danny in high school until he was twenty-one? But no, that hadn't seemed right. They'd trusted their hearts all along. Second-guesses would only weigh them down.

Keeping open minds, Ken and Nancy revisited the possibility of Daniel getting an advanced education. The stumbling block was that he hadn't taken the standardized SATs. The medical and psychological study of traumatic brain injury was in its relative infancy, particularly for young people, and the college admissions tests didn't adequately accommodate students with Daniel's type of memory and information-processing issues. That left him with the options of auditing courses without academic credit or attending them as a non-matriculated student—someone who hasn't been accepted by the school as a regular student, but went on a course-by-course basis, and could earn a limited number of credits toward possible future admission. Either way he'd have to attend classes without a definite path toward earning a college diploma, and that ran strongly against Ken's grain.

Still, he contacted Hofstra and Adelphi Universities on Long Island, Landmark College in Vermont, and Hunter

College in Manhattan, asking about possible programs for special needs students. The advisors at Hunter's Office of AccessABILITY were very helpful and supportive answering questions over the telephone. They explained that there were over five hundred students in their program and offered to meet with Danny at their offices. The Trushes decided to schedule an appointment.

The college's main campus was on Manhattan's Upper Eastside, a conveniently short distance from their apartment. The advisors showed the same courtesy they had on the phone, and gave them a comprehensive overview of their services and assistive technologies for special students. Besides a state-of-the-art computer and study center, they provided one-on-one note takers and a variety of other resources.

All three members of the family were sold on the school. Hunter's inclusiveness of the disabled community and sensitivity toward Daniel's special needs had impressed them.

But for Ken the questions that had hovered over Danny's high school graduation hadn't gone away. What direction was he heading in as a non-matric? What was the plan toward a full degree? *What to do?*

He talked it over with Nancy one evening.

"Why do we need a big plan?" she asked. "We should try to let him build on his strengths."

Ken had looked at her from his living room chair. "But where's Daniel going with it?"

"Let's take it a step at a time," Nancy said. "It's a positive environment. We can see which classes he really enjoys. Watch, listen, talk to him . . . that way we'll find out what subjects he connects with."

"And then?"

"The rest will take care of itself," she said, and smiled. "We need to have faith that something good will happen."

Ken looked at Nancy, thinking. They were jumping into the great unknown. But hadn't Daniel gotten as far as he had on just such leaps of faith? Not only theirs, but leaps across the abyss by his doctors, his therapists, and everyone who loved him? And by his own faith in himself?

Finally he shrugged.

"Sounds like a plan to me," he said.

Freshman orientation at Hunter College in September was a day to remember.

Ken had accompanied Daniel to school, as he would twice a week for the next three years. Although Danny was now out of a wheelchair, he had balance problems and sometimes got confused finding his way around due to his short-term memory losses. Someone had to assist him and, with Nancy back to working fulltime, Ken continued his three-day-a-week schedule at Agency, leaving Tuesdays and Fridays open for Daniel.

Orientation took place in the giant Assembly Hall, and Ken and Daniel made sure to be there. Ken felt pride swelling up in him as he sat beside his son and looked around at the hundreds upon hundreds of students filling the auditorium, knowing Danny was one of them. *A college student!* All his doubts of the previous summer were swept aside by excitement and anticipation. Danny was embarking on a brand-new adventure.

In his first semester, he took a psychology and a music history class. Ken had originally wanted him to enroll for a fuller slate of courses, but Nancy had urged that they go slow. Daniel would have a high volume of homework and study, and he'd require help from his parents. She thought it best to wait and see how much was manageable.

His Music History class had been an easy choice. Fundamentally, Daniel loved music. It had been the irreplaceable thread woven through every stage of his recovery. Around the time he'd been at BOCES, Tamar Martin had recommended a home music therapist named John Marino to the Trushes, thinking Daniel would benefit from his instruction on different levels. Learning an instrument helped with cognition, creativity, and self-expression, improved motor and auditory skills, cultivated a sense of independence, and was a positive alternative to passive activities like watching television or playing computer games. After some quick research, Ken and Nancy had discovered that few things utilized more of the brain than playing music. It required complex processing functions by multiple parts of the brain and had the potential to open up new neural pathways. It nourished, restored, and healed.

The hyper-energetic Marino had clicked with Daniel right off. Ken and Nancy had often heard their singing and laughter from the next room, followed by one of John's emphatic encouragements: "Wow, that was *great!*" He would tell Daniel not to think too much while he played, but to feel the music and make it his own. He'd made each session fun, but it was much, much *more* than fun—John had creative ways of injecting music theory into each lesson. He introduced Daniel to scales, inversions, fingering methods, and the Circle of Fifths. Daniel had thoroughly enjoyed each session and looked forward to the next.

He would now pour himself into his studies at Hunter with similar enthusiasm. His father would bring Danny to school in the late morning for Music History, and he'd meet his volunteer note-taker and go off to class. Then Ken would sit outside the classroom and read until he emerged—always with a big smile on his face.

After Music History, Ken and Daniel would have lunch in the student cafeteria and then head over to the special needs center to prepare for Daniel's psychology class. Daniel had taken so well to his volunteer work at Beth Israel and Rusk, it seemed worth seeing whether he might lean toward a career as a recreational therapy assistant. Psych courses were central to that field of study.

The class was held in a huge lecture hall. Because of its heavy load of reading, writing and memorization, Ken and Nancy had encouraged him to audit it, and find out whether he could handle the coursework, rather than enroll as a non-matric who'd be tested and graded. Free of pressure, Danny was able to relax and fully enjoy the class.

As an auditor, he wasn't assigned a note-taker, so Ken would accompany him into the hall, drop him off in the third or fourth row with a group of students he'd gotten to know, and then take a seat in back. The students liked having Danny in their row and he thrived on their companionship. From the rear of the hall, Ken often saw him raise his hand to ask questions as he'd done before his injury—he had always been the sort of kid who would participate in class.

On the way home, Ken and Daniel often discussed the instructor's lectures and presentations. Ken had been a bit surprised when he realized how completely they had captured his own interest.

Daniel's studies would now take up much of his time. Ken worked with him on his assignments, and he was a willing student. Meanwhile, they kept pushing Danny's body to get stronger. They spent long hours at the gym, and kept up their regular Achilles walks and distance-race training.

Daniel did his sixth Fifth Avenue Mile the same month he started classes at Hunter College. By now his group of power walkers had grown to include Jimmy Mulzet, a forty-six year old mailroom worker at City University who'd been diagnosed with cerebral palsy as an infant. Mulzet's parents had been told he would never walk or be self-sufficient, but he'd defied all his doctors' predictions and succeeded at both. His single-minded goal since 2002 had been to run the famed twenty-six mile New York City Marathon, which he planned to tackle later in the fall.

Mulzet's discipline and ambition had impressed Daniel, who'd been steadily piling up mileage in his workouts. In the back of his mind, he'd begun to wonder if the Marathon, one of the largest in the world, might be achievable for him. But that lofty goal fell into the "maybe someday" category. Fifth Avenue was still his personal yardstick. The year before, he'd brought his time down to sixteen minutes, a long way from the forty-five he had needed to complete the course in 1998. His focus that September remained on improving his pace, and he was now eyeing fifteen minutes.

Daniel finished at 15:50, his best time ever. He was close but not yet there. Although he didn't talk about it, he'd decided he would have to work a little harder for the following year's race.

Daniel found his first semester at Hunter wonderful. He loved being around students his own age and embraced the college environment. But there was a lot of written material for him to digest, volumes of new information. He'd taken the music course as a non-matric—choosing the pass/fail grading option—and his memory issues made it hard for him to keep up.

In spite of his struggles, Daniel got a passing grade in Music History and made his parents proud beyond measure—*he'd earned his first college credits*! But Ken had found his difficulties eye-opening. While he still quietly saw an academic degree as possible for Danny, he acknowledged that expecting him to enroll in more than two classes a semester was unrealistic and unfair.

For the spring 2004 semester, Daniel took sociology and an elementary piano class, registering for both as a non-matriculated student. He eagerly plunged into his studies but sociology proved arduous. The problem was the same one he'd had with psych the semester before. Because of his impaired short-term memory, the prodigious reading, with its treatises, bundles of facts, and names of famous sociologists was draining to him.

Ken and Nancy had mixed feelings when Daniel scored in the 50s and 60s on his midterms. It amounted to a victory of sorts that he was retaining more than half the information on the syllabus. But they knew he was unlikely to pass his final or grade well on his term paper. Although Ken had tried repetition drills and flash cards to help with his memorization, Daniel was becoming frustrated.

The music class proved to be just the right counterbalance. Daniel excelled at the piano. His sight reading, understanding of chord patterns, and technical aptitude for the instrument— he could only play with his right hand—was impressive to his teacher. He'd also shown an exceptional ear and a talent for improvisation.

Delighted, Ken and Nancy saw his success as payoff for the work he'd done with John Marino at home. Danny had always looked forward to those therapy sessions, and his parents had always known he was having fun. But now they had to wonder if music might—just might—hold some special place in his future.

After the sociology midterms, Danny and his parents agreed to change his status in the class to auditor, forgoing the final exam and paper. Ken's eyes had been further opened to the reality that he wasn't yet ready to meet the academic requirements for a bachelor's degree. He would never put a cap on his son's ability to overcome his limitations. But he also realized that if he didn't accept those limitations for what they were, he wouldn't be truly accepting Daniel for the person *he* was.

Danny ended that semester on an overall positive note, with a good feeling about himself, more knowledge than he'd started out with, and precisely what Nancy had hoped he'd derive from college: a chance to build on his strengths.

When the time came to register for the 2004 fall semester, all the new courses Daniel wanted to attend had scheduling conflicts with Ken's work agenda and he considered auditing the piano class again. *Why not?* his parents thought. With his flair for the keyboard, it made sense. The practice and repetition would only help him improve his skills.

But even as Daniel got ready for his third semester at Hunter, he was preparing for a day he'd been focused on for quite a while. The 2004 Fifth Avenue Mile was to be held in mid-August, a month earlier than usual to honor the Summer Olympics in Athens. After completing his last mile, Danny had challenged himself to outdo his previous time records and finally crack fifteen minutes. His right leg paralysis had made it increasingly difficult to lower his pace, but Ken had seen a special determination about him during their workouts and known he was bent on his goal. Daniel had trained hard with regular walking companions, doing hill repeats, distance walks and interval training. For him, surpassing the fifteen-minute mark would be the equivalent of a world class runner breaking a four-minute mile.

That year, Daniel had aimed at a breakthrough. He was no stranger to such things.

Ken had never seen anyone more ready or intense than Daniel on the day of the race.

From the moment the horn went off, he refused to speak to anyone or acknowledge waves and cheers from the crowd with a typical *"Thank you."* There were no easygoing smiles from him. He walked between 3:30 and 3:45 every quarter mile, always focused on his next step, keeping his pace as constant and consistent as possible. He didn't want to waste a breath, or burn a single calorie, with an unnecessary gesture. He was all in, totally committed to his personal mission.

This, Ken knew, was the Daniel that had reached up from the depths of a coma six years before to declare himself present and accounted for.

He completed the race in 14:45, smashing his fifteen-minute record. Raising his arms as he walked past the finish line, he had the small, assured smile of a champion athlete who knew he'd reached a new pinnacle of achievement.

It would be his last Fifth Avenue Mile. He had gotten what he needed from it.

Daniel's daily life was filled with school, music, body strengthening exercises in the gym, and his Achilles walks. He spent time with his family and friends. And he still did his 5Ks. But now he was looking for something more to stoke his competitive fire—a long-term goal that went beyond anything he'd set in the past. It brought up a question that had simmered in the back of his mind since 2003, when Jimmy Mulzet, the marathoner with cerebral palsy, had helped urge and inspire him to improve upon his race time: If he wanted to be the best he could be, shouldn't he take aim at the highest goal possible?

For Daniel, as for racers from all around the planet, that was the New York City Marathon.

––––––––––––––

Throughout the Fall 2004 term at Hunter, Daniel continued to work on his proficiency at the keyboard and grasp of musical concepts. Ken would dutifully wait outside his classroom, reading, thinking and praying as he contemplated his son's future.

Daniel wrapped up the semester drawing a fresh round of positive feedback from his instructor, making it easy for him and his family to decide what course offerings would top their list of preferences for the spring. It was evident to Ken and Nancy that he loved music and was good at it. It was equally clear that his other classes sapped him. Why not encourage him to continue in the direction of his passion?

The next semester, Spring 2005, Daniel enrolled as a nonmatriculated student in a Music Fundamentals course. When the teacher, a young graduate teaching fellow named Stephanie Jensen-Moulton, met him and Ken on the first day of class, it wasn't under the best of circumstances for any of them. In fact, they were all faced with a sticky, unexpected, and, for Stephanie, at least, slightly awkward predicament.

None of them could have imagined how dramatically their lives were about to change.

CHAPTER EIGHTEEN

L ater, Stephanie Jensen-Moulton would say the Trushes were "shiny people." But on that first day of the term, she was only hoping she could make things work for Daniel in her class. It was a touchy proposition.

Stephanie's practice when she started off a new term was to have her students fill out questionnaires that described their musical lives and interests—and whatever else about themselves they wanted to share. It just made sense to get to know them a little and find out what had attracted them to her course.

On his questionnaire, Daniel wrote:

I have a great interest in music and plan to take a number of music classes. I had a brain aneurysm when I was 12 and was in a coma for many days. I never lost my love of music. Before my brain injury, I played the guitar for two years, and the trumpet for two years. Since my injury, I have played the keyboard with my right hand for the last three years.

Stephanie had a relatively high percentage of students with physical and visual disabilities, but she would discover virtually at once that Daniel's multiple issues presented unique challenges. Her initial hint came before he'd ever set foot in her classroom, when his assigned note-taker told Stephanie that she felt unprepared to write the basic musical notation the course would require. She simply wasn't familiar with it, and was tactfully suggesting she wanted to be removed.

That left Stephanie in a bind. She recognized that not all note takers had a background in the subject being studied, and understood why the volunteer might be skittish. Still, what was her new student going to do? Daniel *needed* class notes.

Although she hadn't yet realized it, the answer was standing right outside her door. Stephanie's conversation with the note-taker had occurred as Daniel was entering the classroom, and his father, who'd been waiting outside, had overheard it.

Ken Trush immediately introduced himself to Stephanie. In an agreeable tone, he explained that Daniel had short-term memory loss that sometimes caused him to become disoriented, that he was "on hand to assist his son getting to and from classes," and that he'd "stayed out of the classroom because he wanted Daniel's participation to be as independent as possible."

With the note-taker bowing out, Ken proposed that he do the job himself. He assured Stephanie that he'd take a seat in the back of the classroom rather than sit up front with his son. He didn't want to interfere with her lessons, and promised to be as unobtrusive as possible. His only other associated request was that Stephanie allow him to record the lessons on tape. Repetition helped Daniel retain information, and he thought he might play them back at home. He'd also privately wondered if Daniel would find it easier processing information delivered by auditory means than through written materials. His ability to quickly memorize music, lyrics and scales had made Ken hopeful it would work.

At first, Stephanie hesitated to accept. She'd never had the parent of one of her students sit in on a class, and was uncomfortable with the idea. But, as she would subsequently write, "if I waited for the college to assign a new note-taker, Daniel could lose weeks of class notes in the process. Consequently I welcomed Ken into my classes."

He kept his end of their bargain, going out of his way not to be a distraction to her or the students. During class Stephanie would notice him sitting quietly back with his notepad and tape recorder. "Daniel did not acknowledge his father's presence ..." she wrote, "but rather sat in the front row, middle seat, generally participating enthusiastically."

His enthusiasm did not, however, translate into high marks on his quizzes and exams. Stephanie had tried to be proactive accommodating his disabilities, discussing various methods and strategies with Ken early in the semester. Since Daniel's visual tracking sometimes gave him problems, they decided he would use a magnifying sheet with his textbooks. Stephanie found he had no trouble reading her whiteboards from his vantage at the front of the room.

But Daniel still wasn't doing well on his quizzes. Part of the problem was that he wasn't finishing them despite being given twice the usual time permitted students. "When asked to do a series of the same type of task, such as writing a Major third above the given note, Daniel would seem to have completed the first problem several times, erasing the same answer over and over again, and rewriting it," she observed.

What puzzled Stephanie was that his homework assignments were all complete, as opposed to the quizzes. Asking Ken and Daniel about it, she discovered that Daniel could become disoriented during tasks and forget when he'd already concluded one. "At home," she wrote, "Daniel's family would help him remember where he was in the task, and would tell him to move forward. In tests, he would think he had completed a section, but no one was there to tell him he had not finished the work."

As she grew to know Daniel, Stephanie came to wish she'd had a better understanding of his disabilities out of the gate. Here was a determined, courageous young man who had survived five brain aneurysms, re-learned how to walk, talk, and write. His music therapist John Marino had taught him to play the piano with his right hand, while using the index finger of his spastic left to tap out accompaniments on the bass keys. If she was going to fairly serve Daniel as an educator, Stephanie told herself she "needed to find a solution that would help him get through the tests in a way that really evaluated his abilities, but without giving him any advantage over the other students."

Stephanie would try assorted techniques, from spacing the test questions apart in vertical columns so Daniel could more easily see which ones he'd answered, to having him use sticky notes to actually cover his answers as he entered them. No single method was altogether successful—but by his midterms Daniel's grades had improved. That seemed to light him up. His subsequent quiz scores climbed and he earned a passing grade for the class.

Excited about what Daniel had accomplished that semester, Stephanie decided to invite him to take her more advanced ear training course in the fall. He had a very good ear, and she wanted to work with that and see where it led. Now that she'd gained a stronger awareness of his needs—and a clearer picture of his attributes—who could say what she'd bring out of him?

She decided to approach Ken with the idea on the last day of classes.

"Daniel's doing really well and competing along with the other students," Stephanie said. "He has a very good musical ear, close to perfect pitch. I'd love for him to join me in my ear training class next semester."

Smiling, Ken stood beside Daniel in the hallway outside her classroom. Her words had left him thunderstruck. He'd almost felt the lightning snap through his mind. He half expected SJM, as Stephanie's students called her, to sniff the ozone in the air around him.

Throughout the semester, Ken had checked in with her to keep tabs on his son's progress. She'd always been positive and motivating when she discussed Danny's attributes with him, while being direct about areas that needed improvement. She'd been honest in every instance. That was something you picked up about her right off. SJM came to work decked out in honesty.

Ken would have had a hard time distilling his feelings at that moment into a single word. From Daniel's first semester at Hunter, he and Nancy had committed to following his lead, to letting his passion and interest guide them all. For Ken it had meant fully surrendering to faith and acceptance, just as he had when he'd played his CDs at Daniel's bedside years before, singing along that he would never give up on him. Just as he had when he thought of the words to his good-night song, and then when he'd sung his oldies to draw Daniel's voice from wherever it had been trapped inside him. Each time, Ken had believed—no, that wasn't quite it—each time, he'd *allowed himself to accept* the belief that the pieces would fall together. Things would work out.

These past couple of years at college, music had been Daniel's invariable compass point, the shore toward which he'd naturally sailed. But what possibilities for his future might music contain? To Ken it was always the central question. Daniel's previous music instructors at Hunter had said encouraging things. They had brought Daniel and his family closer to an answer. But until now it had felt as if they were still walking around its periphery. Stephanie Jensen-Moulton had opened the door and invited them in.

Validated. If Ken had to choose a word for how he felt, that would have been it. He and Nancy had put their hearts in line behind Daniel's, letting him be their guide. And it had been the best choice they could have made.

"What do you say, Danny?" he asked, turning to him. "It's your decision. Think you want to take Stephanie's class?"

Daniel looked at her. "Sure," he said slowly. "I'd love it, SJM. Thank you for asking me."

Stephanie smiled. "Thank *you*, Daniel."

Lightning, Ken thought. She'd sparked lightning in his head and heart. Like magic.

Taking hold of Danny's elbow, Ken walked him down the hall toward the elevator. He could hardly wait to tell Nancy what he was thinking.

As he sat typing at his home computer, Ken mused that he would have been stranded without Internet search engines. If there was inspiration behind every great idea, then you could also count on having a multitude of questions and details along with it. He had known it when he'd told Nancy about his brainstorm at Hunter College, the basics of which had virtually poured from his lips without a breath between words: That Daniel find a life path that would bring his love of music, and everything it meant to his ongoing journey, to the journeys of others with disabilities.

Nancy had jumped on board at once. But she'd pointed out that the idea was very broad. How was Daniel going to make it a reality? Ken hadn't had the answer. He didn't know what channels were available to their son. Finding out, then, would be their obvious starting point.

Ken had been obsessed with that in the week or so since, using every available moment for his research. He'd already gone through several terms in his current session. There had been *music for people with disabilities, music for people with disabilities in New York City, music therapy* . . .

Ken considered that last one. Music therapy was an interesting field, and Daniel's experience with John Marino had resoundingly confirmed its benefits. But therapy was usually given one-on-one and tailored to a client's individual goals. While many of its aspects were compatible with Ken's idea, it wouldn't reach the large cross-section of people he envisioned. And because of Daniel's physical and cognitive challenges, there were a slew of reasons why it didn't hold career possibilities for him. Whatever direction he took would require teamwork, the assistance and involvement of those to whom he was closest. He would need his family beside him.

What next? *What to do?*

Ken thought about it. Daniel was a living example of what could be attained by someone with a disability. Over the past few years, he'd done periodic speaking engagements at the request of different parties. Tamar Martin had invited him and Ken to speak to a college class she'd taught. They had visited a public school in Queens, a BOCES school, a Christian mission in lower Manhattan . . . even a TBI conference in Albany. As Daniel had gotten more skilled at the keyboard, he'd performed at some of his appearances. He'd always gotten a warm reception from his audiences.

The talks had been gratifying. Daniel and Ken had wanted to share the miracle their family had received, hoping it could uplift and inspire others who were going through their own personal challenges. It had also felt rewarding to educate people about TBI. But those appearances were infrequent, and after a while Ken and Daniel had felt as if the talks weren't enough. They'd wanted to make a broader impact on their community.

Now Ken leaned forward in his chair and input more search terms, adding new keywords. The phrases *music education/individuals with disabilities* were coupled together in several of the results that came up. They intrigued him, bringing to mind larger groups of people, classroom situations . . . might Daniel find a role within such a setting? Maybe as part of a team?

Ken clicked onto one website after another. He found a number of solid educational programs, but each was geared toward people with a specific disability. While he didn't see anything wrong with that approach, he was looking for something more inclusive. He and Daniel remembered the impatient frowns they'd gotten from fellow passengers on city buses when Danny had to be loaded aboard in his wheelchair. To the people who knew him, Daniel was a hero. To some who didn't, and who hadn't had interactions with a disabled person, he was damaged. He had a firsthand understanding of the rejection people with impairments experienced. He'd felt the sting of being marginalized. There were fifty million disabled people in the United States—one in six. Of those individuals, half had severe disabilities, meaning they needed some form of assistance in their daily living activities. Why leave anyone out?

Stymied, Ken expelled a breath. He and his family were neophytes at what they were trying to do. And what exactly *was* that? What direction should they take?

Maybe, Ken thought, he needed to take a step backward. Whenever he did an analysis and assessment of corporate objectives for Agency, he laid them out in writing. It made sense to do that now. List their goals, and then formulate a plan for executing them. In short, create a family mission statement. If they were going to find their purpose, it would happen by revisiting their starting point: the details and questions that followed inspiration.

———————

Ken and Nancy had reserved one evening of the week as their date night, starting back when Danny was at The Smith School, and Ken had reduced his schedule at Agency. If he spent Friday afternoons with Danny, and Saturday Mornings with Mike, then the nights he and Nancy reserved for themselves had their own special quality. They did what sweethearts did together, having quiet dinners out, going on unhurried walks, occasionally taking in a movie or Broadway play.

In the month or so after Ken's pivotal moment at Hunter, they talked about it a great deal on their date nights. At other times, they discussed the subject with Daniel, or Mike, or both their sons at once. Mike, who was now seventeen, and aspiring toward a career in child psychology, had no shortage of input.

Ken would write everything down as they probed their intentions and tried to identify their ideals, principles and values. He would scrutinize every objective on their evolving list, delve into their reasons for considering it, ask probing questions of himself and the rest of the family. Is this honestly what we believe? Would that help anyone? How? Is it attainable? Does it fall in with our core goals? Ideas were added and subtracted, revised and sometimes discarded.

The document he wound up with looked like this:

What Do We Stand For?

1). *Use music for self-expression, creativity and enjoyment.*
2). *Use music for performance*: Daniel loves playing the keyboard and showing the progress he's made. Why not show everybody the multiple talents of individuals with disabilities?
3). *Use music as a tool for celebration of the individual*: With all the therapies people with disabilities undertake to get better, shouldn't every individual have a place to celebrate who he or she is today? Where just being oneself is good enough?
4). *Use music for fun*: Music is a universal language. Almost everybody loves it in some capacity. How about making it a positive and joyful means for helping to relax and smile?
5). *Use music to bring people together*: Socialization in a group environment is important. True socialization conquers isolation and rejection. We are fundamentally social beings, yet individuals with disabilities spend much of their time isolated or working one-on-one with

therapists. Wouldn't group classes for the disabled be beneficial?

6). *Use music to learn*: Studies indicate that singing and playing music are among the most mentally complex activities, as they utilize many different parts of the brain. Doesn't that necessarily develop and improve the total being?

With his family's aims and aspirations roughly declared on paper, Ken launched into the work of finding an organization that might embrace and advance their mission. He spoke to music therapists, music educators, foundation officers and community outreach coordinators, and even visited a music therapy center.

The more Ken searched, asked, probed, learned, weighed, and then discussed with Nancy, the more they grew convinced that none of the established programs was quite the right fit for them.

It made their next decision easy.

If the program didn't exist, they'd just create one themselves.

———————

But what to call it?

Ken had been in the business world long enough to know that if you were going to start an organization, it was wise to incorporate from the get-go. And before you incorporated, you had to give the organization a name.

He spoke with Chan Suh, his partner at Agency, asking if he had any suggestions. Chan figured a good springboard would be the family's mission statement, but felt they should pare it down to basics so it was firmly embedded in their minds—and could be easily communicated to other people. It would be their clarion, their call to action, and their calling card. After giving it some thought, what he came up with was: "Provide a comfortable, educational and social environment in which our members can enjoy, learn and practice the joy of music together."

The Trushes agreed they loved his language. It seemed to say it all. Except that the sentence was missing an opening clause. And a name for the organization.

The name game quickly became their family preoccupation. It went on over breakfast, lunch and dinner, while they were watching television or getting ready for bed, taking walks or drives, or even just hanging around the little playground area outside their apartment building.

"Music for Life?" Ken wondered quietly.

"Music for Everyone?" Nancy wondered.

"Music for All," Mike said.

"How about Music for Joy?" Danny asked.

For various reasons none of the names worked. Most didn't get across quite the right message. Ken found many of the better considerations already taken when he checked them out online. The family kept sorting through different possibilities.

One weekday after school, they all sat down at the dining room table to bat around ideas. Grandma Eva happened to have stopped by for a visit, and heard them getting a bit wound up. They just couldn't seem to find what they wanted.

"Music for the Pros!" she offered, cutting in.

They all turned their heads to look at her.

"Music for the Pros?" Ken said.

Eva nodded in her imperturbable way.

A moment later they were all laughing uproariously. The name she'd come with was absurdly contrary to everything the family wanted their program to stand for, making her message clear: *Relax. Let it come naturally. Don't obsess.*

They took her implied advice and let it go for the rest of that afternoon.

————————————

Ken ran some of their potential names by Chan, sounding lukewarm about them even as they left his mouth.

"Ken," Chan said pointedly after listening to him awhile. "This program . . . why are you doing it? What's your *vision?*"

Ken thought about it. "Daniel loves music," he replied after a moment. "It gives him joy, it's brought him confidence, and it's helped him feel accepted. It's been a powerful healing force for him ever since his injury, and he wants to share it with other people who face the challenges of living with disabilities."

Chan nodded. "Then why not keep it simple?" he said. "If Daniel is the inspiration and catalyst, why not call it Daniel's Music Foundation?"

Ken looked at him a long time. Then looked at him some more. The idea was simplicity itself. And it had been right there in front of him all along.

"Chan," he said at last, smiling. "You're the definition of genius."

CHAPTER NINETEEN

I t would be half a year before the Trushes were able to start the process of bringing Daniel's Music Foundation from conception to reality.

In late 2005, they lost all three of their family elders in the space of a month, Grandma Eva and Grandma Jeanne in November, and Grandpa Pepe on the first day of December. As their parents ailed throughout the summer and fall, Ken and Nancy had put their plans for DMF on the backburner to care for them. While recovering from their losses, the Trushes were well served by the essential lesson they'd learned from their experience with Daniel: You had to move forward, inch by inch, with faith and perseverance. It was all anyone could do.

The New Year brought their focus back to the nascent foundation. It helped with the family's healing. They entered 2006 with a sense of renewal and hope for the future.

By midwinter the Trushes had put several key ingredients for DMF into the mix. They'd registered it as a nonprofit and received some startup donations from friends and relatives. A long conversation with John Marino, Danny's music therapist, had convinced him to climb on board. Marino, in turn, referred them to a colleague who headed a large music therapy center on Long Island, thinking he might be able to help them develop their program. He would provide valuable advice early on as a paid consultant.

From DMF's inception, the Trushes had decided not to take any form of financial compensation out of its funding. They felt that generosity, trust and belief in others was contagious. If they gave of themselves, and trusted their members, they were convinced people would do their best to reciprocate. Program offerings would be free; if a member chose to make a donation, every penny would be applied to operational costs. The Trushes understood everyone wouldn't respond that way but thought the majority of people would. Trust and a sense of community had bolstered their spirits when Daniel was clinging to life by a thread, and they would stand behind those values building the foundation.

With their charter drawn up, the next step was to find a site where they could hold classes. Ken and Nancy discovered just the right place walking home from a restaurant on their regular date night. Or actually rediscovered it. Coincidentally or not, they'd been there thirty years before—on a date.

Back then the place had been the site of Wednesday's disco, one of three hot dance clubs on East Eighty-Sixth Street in the city's Yorkville neighborhood. There had been Barney Googles a block west near Lexington Avenue, and the Corso Latin Ballroom off the corner of Third Avenue, and Wednesday's between Second and Third, a large underground space laid out to resemble a village street, its long main "avenue" running past barrooms and dance floors.

Now it hardly bore a resemblance to the nightspot where Ken and Nancy had gone for their third night out as boyfriend and girlfriend. As they walked by, hand-in-hand, they almost hadn't recognized it. The awning above its nondescript entrance read Go Fish! Studios, and a flyer on the glass door had an announcement about special needs programs. That was what caught Ken's eye, the sign. As he stopped to read it, he noticed a descending flight of stairs on the other side of the door. Wednesday's had had the same type of stairway leading down to the action on its lower level.

"Nancy," Ken said, "Is *this* . . .?"

"I think it is," she said.

Ken exchanged glances with her, smiled, and opened the door. What they'd read on the flyer had intrigued them. As they went downstairs, they knew for certain they were in space once occupied by the disco. The whirling lights had been replaced with plain fluorescent overheads, the throbbing music by a quietly bubbling fish tank facing the entry, and the coat check by a small reception area at the foot of the stairs. But it was the same place.

Asking a pleasant man at the front desk what went on at Go Fish!, Ken and Nancy were told it was a special needs center with classes and activities for autistic children. Ken's mental gears instantly started to turn. He'd noticed a spacious studio— once part of the dance floor—through a glass wall to the right of the reception area. The receptionist explained that there was a second studio beyond it.

"Do you ever rent them out?" Ken inquired.

Yes, in fact, they did, in certain situations, the receptionist replied, glad to let Ken and Nancy have a look around. They walked past the glass wall, turned down an aisle to the right, and saw the other studio. It was about the same size as the first. Intrigued by the possibilities, they returned to the front desk and took a business card.

Ken called the next day and arranged to meet with two of the space's owners. The rest happened quickly. He and Danny went over together, explained what they were trying to do, and were offered Friday nights at a moderate rate. Ken's heart raced. They were ready to go.

Well, mostly ready. They still hadn't decided on a class offering. They didn't know what equipment they'd need for it. And it was a wide-open question whether anyone in the disabled community would be interested in their foundation.

Small steps, Ken reminded himself. The Friday night slot booked, he wasted no time getting in touch with John Marino.

The truth was they didn't have much to discuss. Danny had studied the piano with Marino, and that had launched him into taking keyboards in college. The joy and healing he'd gotten out of it, the acceptance he'd gained from socializing at school, and the desire to bring that feeling to other people, had been the trifecta of inspirations for DMF. What could have been more appropriate than a keyboard class?

Marino agreed to teach it, and that was that.

Two down, Ken thought.

Now for the instruments.

Sam Ash on Forty-Eighth Street was one of the largest, oldest, and most famous music stores in the country. The Trushes headed over there on a Sunday afternoon with barely a clue about what to purchase—or even what questions to ask. They wanted to buy several electronic keyboards. But which brand? How fancy did they have to be? What was a fair price?

All they knew for sure was that they weren't leaving without them.

After consulting with the sales manager, they decided on Yamaha starter keyboards. At a hundred-fifty dollars each, the cost seemed reasonable. And when the manager heard about their foundation and set them up with a running store discount, the deal got even better.

They drove home from Sam Ash with a half dozen keyboards in very bulky cardboard packaging boxes cramming their car.

Three down.

DMF's first class would be held on Friday, March 3, 2006. The Trushes and John Marino eagerly planned for it, mindful of their core criteria: they wanted people to socialize, learn, and above all else have fun. With his "Feel the music" axiom and kinetic personality, Marino was just the right teacher.

But how to measure the success of DMF once it launched? How to assess goals and outcomes? At one of several meetings at his apartment, Ken turned to his business background for answers. The return on investment, or ROI, was the most fundamental mathematical gauge of a company's baseline performance, he explained. Key success factors, or KSFs, as well as key performance indicators—KPIs—were also highly useful analytical tools.

"Dad?" Sitting at the dining room table, Daniel had listened quietly to the entire session, taking it all in.

Ken waited.

"I want to use a 'Smile-o-meter,'" Danny said. "I want to judge success based on the number of smiles we get."

Ken hardly knew how to respond. Danny was also calculating investment versus returns. His metrics had nothing to do with finances, though. They stemmed from his personal experiences with therapy, trying to feel better, and gaining acceptance. And he was right. Of course DMF had to stay solvent. It needed to serve and grow its membership within a responsible financial framework. But the return they sought on its investments was to enrich the heart and soul, and to uplift the spirit. If it succeeded at those things, it would have met its paramount goals.

"Okay, Danny," Ken said. "The Smile-o-meter it'll be."

That made everyone in the room smile. Naturally.

Next came the all-important question of how to spread awareness about DMF. Before anybody signed up for classes, they obviously had to know the foundation existed. Given its tight budget and grassroots philosophy, word of mouth seemed the best route. But how to get a buzz going?

The Trushes tossed around ideas with their friends and advisors, and eventually decided to hold monthly Music Appreciation events to bring people together, explain what DMF was all about, and perhaps someday showcase the talents of individuals with disabilities. Attendance would be free, with donations accepted. A hundred guests seemed a good target audience—not too big, not too small—and they called around for spaces that could hold a group that size.

Ken and Nancy found a gem in the Church of St. Jean Baptiste, a landmark neighborhood church with which their family had a long history. Nancy had gone to its Catholic school, she and Ken had gotten married there, and it had been the church where both boys were baptized. Besides all that, St. Jean's price was right, and the parish had just renovated its basement community center. It seemed perfect.

They reserved the room for February 26, the Sunday before their flagship course was scheduled at Go Fish!. The performance would feature their friends Kathy Lord and Susan Weber, who'd formed a partnership called Music that Heals to bring their talents to seriously ill kids in hospitals and other healthcare facilities. Kathy and Susan had played for Daniel when he was emerging from his coma at Beth Israel, and then again at the Rusk Institute, and the Trushes had never forgotten it. They left the entertainment program entirely up to them.

On Saturday, Ken and Nancy scrambled to Costco for food—and plenty of it. Cheese and crackers, fruit, vegetables, dip, cookies, and cream puffs—would anyone be able to resist free *cream puffs*?

The event's turnout was fantastic. The room was crowded with friends, friends of friends, and acquaintances the Trushes had met through Beth Israel, Rusk, Achilles and Mount Sinai Medical Center, where Daniel had attended the Phase II program. People danced and sang along to the music, and many signed up for membership—among them Artie Elefant, Jimmy Mulzet, and Nadine and Tyler McNeil from Achilles.

The word about DMF had been put out in celebratory fashion, and everyone loved the cream puffs.

John Marino's inaugural class was a success. It was filled to capacity—five students sat at five of the starter keyboards, and Marino had the sixth. Daniel would notice that the Smile-o-Meter readings soared sky-high that day.

As Ken later reflected, they were off to the races.

PART FOUR

MARATHON MOM (AND CHICKEN SOUP)

CHAPTER TWENTY

It was 6:15 AM on Sunday, November 4, 2007.

Ken Trush sat looking out his window into the predawn twilight, Daniel quiet beside him as their bus rumbled south on the East River Drive toward the Battery Tunnel. The taillights of the bus up ahead were faint dabs of red in the windshield, the headlights of their trailing bus much brighter as they cast their horizontal beams through the rear window. The three buses were part of a caravan strung out along the highway, carrying hundreds of disabled athletes and volunteers to Staten Island, where they would gather at the starting line for the New York City Marathon.

Their stomachs filled with butterflies, Ken and Daniel had slept very little despite having gone into bed early the night before. As they'd dressed at 4:30 AM, Ken had imagined he felt something like a fight trainer preparing a boxer for a championship bout. He'd smeared Vaseline on Danny's chest to prevent chafing from his tee shirt, helped him put on his numbered bib, and then carefully pulled his shoelaces through the hard plastic disc imbedded with a computer chip for marking his time. What would the day be like for them? he'd wondered. Would Danny cross the finish line smiling or grimacing in agony? If he wasn't able to go the distance, would they wonder if they'd missed something in preparation? And what if Danny got hurt? Would he, Ken, be able to look Nancy in the eye feeling they'd made the right decision? Or would he be remorseful for having persuaded her to go along with it?

Ken had known he'd get his answers soon enough. But right then he'd only had the nerves, excitement, and anticipation in the pit of his stomach.

By five o'clock, he and Danny had done their leg stretches, shrugged into their backpacks, and been ready to leave. They'd had to catch the special bus departing from midtown half an hour later. Kate Parkin, who'd been Danny's ICU therapist at Beth Israel, and had trained with him for the past six months, would meet them there, as would Chloe Malle, an Achilles volunteer who'd become a close friend and Marathon teammate. Dave Wolf would join them later on, as would, Daniel's cousin Ted Upson, another member of their team. And then Mike at the halfway point of the race.

As they walked out the door, Ken had prayed they would walk back in safe and victorious.

He continued to gaze outside now as the bus neared the entrance to the Battery Tunnel. If he looked hard through the gloom to his left, he could see the piers of southern Manhattan extended over the river like concrete fingers. And across the river, high above the Brooklyn waterfront, the industrial smokestacks with their aircraft warning lights winking in the dark.

Ten years ago, Ken thought, he wouldn't have imagined taking this ride with Daniel. Ten years ago, Danny had still been at Rusk on a feeding tube, barely able to walk a few feet out of his wheelchair. But today he would shoot for half of the Marathon's full twenty-six miles on his legs, and the rest on a handcrank bike. *Twenty-six miles.*

It already had been quite a journey. For Daniel, for the rest of the family, and for the foundation born of Danny's inextinguishable light and spirit.

Over the past eighteen months, DMF had grown from John Marino's single keyboard class to *nine* classes, with two new teachers coming on—a therapist and educator named Jaime Lyn Palmer, and, to the Trushes' surprise, Stephanie Jensen-Moulton, Daniel's professor at Hunter, who'd agreed to teach courses when her academic career allowed. As word of mouth spread from member to member, parent to parent, and then to service coordinators for people with disabilities, the foundation had added voice and children's instruction courses to the program. The Music Appreciation events at St. Jean's community center had blossomed into semi-annual Music Celebration concerts, with Nancy preparing food in the kitchen before shows, and rushing upstairs with Ken to bring DMF members down as they arrived on special Access-a-ride vehicles, and Mike dashing around to set up all the instruments and equipment they brought over from Go Fish!, running cables and electrical cords everywhere. Danny would greet people as they came in, and Mike would be the human public address system, holding up a boom box for sound. And then there was the cleanup afterward.

It was at once exhausting and exhilarating. Daniel's recovery from his injury had been so incremental and slow that the accelerated growth of DMF over the past year had often made Ken and Nancy feel like they were trying to hang onto the tail of a barreling jet plane. But they'd understood that in both cases it was all about love, giving, trusting their hearts, and finally having the faith to relinquish control to a Higher Will.

Meanwhile, Daniel had been training for a new athletic goal. After breaking his fifteen minute record in the 2004 Fifth Avenue Mile, he'd asked Ken whether the New York City Marathon was a realistic ambition, and they'd formulated a progressive multi-year plan that would gradually prepare him for it—and alleviate Nancy's concerns that he might be pushing his body too far, in too short a time. In 2005 he'd walked the last ten miles of the Marathon after months of tough conditioning, blisters, blackened toenails, and broken leg braces. In 2006, Danny had increased his distance to 13.1 miles, and felt he was ready to train for the entire course.

Nancy had again expressed some misgivings. The course would take nine hours and put his metabolism on overdrive. What would be the long-term effects on his legs and joints? He compensated for his paralyzed leg with his left when he walked . . . might he damage that one too?

Ken and Daniel decided on a team approach to address her questions. They consulted with the pediatric podiatrist Dr. Paul Jordan, who specialized in neurological impairments that affected children's mobility. Jordan had treated Daniel after his injury, and agreed with Nancy that the twenty-six miles might, in fact, be pushing the limit. He suggested that Daniel carry a replacement leg brace in the eventuality that the one he wore broke. When Ken and Daniel spoke to Dick Traum, the founder of Achilles, he'd raised the possibility of Daniel using a handcrank bike instead of walking the course—but they hadn't seen it as an option. He'd walked half the distance the year before. Why shoot for less?

In the end they combined the two men's advice. Daniel would walk as much as he could and use a custom built handcrank to help him go the distance. He'd also have a second brace as backup.

When Ken and Daniel had considered their emergency planning, they'd immediately thought of Kate Parkin. She knew Daniel's physical capabilities as well as anyone and had run a dozen Marathons, only stopping because of ankle issues. Having kept in touch with her over the years, they'd given her a ring.

"We're going to do the Marathon," Ken said. "Will you do it with us? Will you help train us and do it?"

Shot ankles or not, Kate hadn't hesitated. She'd seen Daniel move his big toe for the first time after he awakened from his coma, she would later recall. How could she have refused? Kate would take a highly detailed approach to the training, and had even researched the road gradient of each mile of the race to help determine where Daniel would walk or use the handcrank.

An Achilles volunteer named Michael Oliva had completed a number of fifty and one-hundred mile ultramarathons, and Ken and Daniel had turned to him for information about how to fuel Danny's body. Oliva had suggested a list of fruits and vegetable products, but cautioned that every person was different, and that a marathoner should never try new foods during a race. Daniel and Ken would choose peanut butter on bagels to provide protein and carbohydrates, bananas for potassium, and plenty of water and Snapple Grapeade for fluids and sugar. Oliva also suggested chicken soup as a way to rapidly get fat, carbs, protein and salt into the system, and they'd taken note.

Finally, they had asked Dave and Chloe—and then Ted—to join their team. Would they be up to sharing in the excitement? They'd readily counted themselves in.

Daniel's intensive training had started in April. It was months of disciplined training on the handcrank and workout machines, of stretching and walking and consistently adding to his mileage totals, of pain and soreness and determination.

And now, Ken thought, here they were. On the bus to Staten Island before sunrise, their backpacks in front of their feet. Danny had his name on his bib along with his number; Kate, Chloe, and his Achilles volunteers the words "Go Danny" on theirs.

Go Danny Go.

Part of Ken could hardly believe it. But another part of him wasn't surprised. If Daniel had proven anything in his life, it was that he was never to be underestimated.

Ken broke from his reverie as the bus swung out of the tunnel. He could see the lower Manhattan skyline to his right across the bay, the first light of day spreading over its glass-and-steel financial towers like glowy paint. Up ahead dawn dappled the water with orange and gold.

That early sunshine put a lump in his throat. He couldn't have articulated why. But he noticed many of the other runners on the bus looking out their windows with set, purposeful expressions on their faces, and guessed their thoughts and feelings weren't so different from his. Each had a story, a personal reason for doing the Marathon, a driving force within that had compelled him or her to take on its formidable twenty-six miles.

As they rolled closer to Staten Island, all of them looked ready.

The New York Road Runners Club organized the Marathon, and its rules permitted an early start for walkers with disabilities who would need extra time to finish the course—and a slightly later advance start for elite runners and wheelchair division racers so they could compete without being slowed by the main crowd.

At 8:00 AM, two hours before a round of cannon fire officially began the race for thousands, the less dramatic blast of
an air horn would signal its commencement for the fifty or so
disabled athletes gathered ahead of the pack at the foot of the
Verrazano-Narrows Bridge.

Ken approached the starting line with Daniel and their
friends. He'd been observing the people around him, studying
their preparations, their varied demeanors. Some were giddy
with excitement, some silent and introspective, while some just
seemed quietly confident. Ken had supposed he and Danny fell
into the latter category. They felt very prepared.

After several minutes, Ken's thoughts had been interrupted by
hugs and good wishes from his teammates, and then they'd all
assembled at the line. Waiting for their signal, Ken once again
felt the butterflies swirling around inside him. He exchanged
nods and smiles with other athletes, waved to a few of the race
officials. He would remember that the air was cool, the full
morning sun bright in the sky.

Then the horn sounded. Team Danny started toward the
bridge. The Marathon was on.

Spanning the Bay of New York from north to south, the two-
mile length of the Verrazano Bridge was closed to regular vehic-
ular traffic for the race. The small number of disabled athletes
started across it, rooting loudly for each other as they walked
their first yards.

With the day's high temperature predicted to be in the midfif-
ties, Daniel and Ken had worn extra layers of clothing, but they
would now peel them off their perspiring bodies as they went
uphill and then downhill over the bridge's curving main deck.

Strong and beaming with assurance, Daniel was in his glory. Buses carrying elite runners to the starting line went slowly in the opposite direction, and he smiled and greeted them with waves. The Achilles volunteers kept a close eye on his pace; one of their many responsibilities was to see that he didn't start out—and risk burning out—too fast. On Kate's suggestion, Team Danny was aiming for twenty-minute walking miles and about fifteen minutes per mile on the handcrank. With bathroom breaks, and stops for stretching and replenishment of nutrients, they hoped to finish in about eight hours.

Daniel made it over the bridge and onto Fourth Avenue in Bay Ridge, Brooklyn, without problems. The avenue was a long, flat stretch, and Kate had calculated it would be a good one for eating up miles while the disabled athletes had the road to themselves.

Danny moved smoothly, his team pausing every mile to drink and have some solid food. His early choice was the peanut butter and bagel combo; Michael Oliva had told him and Ken—and Kate reminded them—that protein took longer to digest, and was best eaten near the beginning of the course.

With the main crowd of runners still an hour away from their start only a smattering of people had lined up behind the curbside barricades on Fourth Avenue, giving Daniel an opportunity to thank each one of them as he passed. At Mile Three, he spotted the familiar faces of Uncle Steve and Aunt Debbie, who lived in Bay Ridge, among the spectators. Their lively high-fives, hugs and cheers gave him and his teammates a boost of energy.

They pressed ahead. Another mile went by, another, two more. At Mile Eight the crowds along the sidewalk thickened. The elite marathoners and wheelchair athletes were catching up to the original fifty disabled walkers, coming on in a swift, rushing wave.

Ken's eyes grew large as the wave overtook him. Here they came, the wheelchair racers, their faces masks of effort and concentration, their upper arms bulging as they worked their hand rims. And here were the lead runners, close-up now, the most well-tuned in the world. Lean and rangy, they moved as effortlessly and gracefully as thoroughbreds with their long, beautiful strides.

Ken and Daniel watched them go by. The best in the world, the best, and Team Danny was in *the same race!* The thought left them breathless with wonder and awe.

It also excited the onlookers. The sidewalk crowds were getting larger and louder, chanting "GO DANNY GO! GO DANNY GO!" at the top of their lungs as Daniel either reached them on foot holding his father's arm, or wheeled by them gripping his handcrank.

When he heard their cheers and applause, Daniel, true to his nature, tried his hardest to thank them all.

Daniel hit his first ebb eleven miles in, as the team approached the Pulaski Bridge in Queens. Ken and their volunteers had already noticed he'd been asking for a bathroom stop every half hour, which wasn't a great sign. If Danny couldn't retain water it would seriously jeopardize his chances of finishing the race. And now his stamina seemed to be fading.

Ken gave him more than a few bananas to eat and switched him from water to Snapple Grapeade, thinking the fluid, sugar, and vitamins would raise his energy level. That seemed to do the trick for a while, but he soon began looking fatigued again.

Ken could only hope Daniel would get another lift when he saw his brother. Anticipating Danny might tire around the halfway point, Mike had concluded it would be the right place to join the team, and he did at Mile Thirteen near the ramp for the Fifty-ninth Street Bridge. Daniel perked up when he saw him appear from the crowd with his Go Danny shirt and runner's pass, smiling his enthusiastic smile.

But Daniel had gone a considerable distance on his feet. He needed to conserve his resources and give his legs a rest. As the team turned onto the bridge to cross the East River into Manhattan they'd noticed at once that it was very quiet, with no spectators lining its deck to pull for the runners. That also seemed to lower Daniel's energy reserves. Taking those factors into consideration, everyone felt it would be best for him to use the handcrank.

The idea made basic sense. But it didn't work out.

The hitch was the massive number of runners coming off the Manhattan side of the bridge onto First Avenue. Amid the close press of human bodies, Daniel had to struggle to maneuver the bike, and the focus and effort he needed to steer and brake was visibly draining to him. Danny had seemed much more fluid and comfortable on his feet.

And so, a reversal of plans—there would be more walking and less handcranking. But how would he hold up?

As Danny and his group continued along First Avenue, the welcome from the crowd was deafening—a sharp contrast with the total quiet behind them. Suddenly they had walls of people on either side again, and it gave everyone on the team an adrenaline rush.

Unfortunately it didn't sustain Daniel for long. He was physically depleted. About a half mile up the avenue, at the sixteen mile marker, he started showing signs of real distress. His face had paled, his shoulders were slumped forward, and he wasn't responding to spectators. The extra walking had made him perspire far more heavily than he would have with the hand-crank, and that had left him in danger of becoming dehydrated. He didn't look as if he'd make it to the finish.

Ken reached for his cell phone. Nancy would be waiting at Ninetieth Street and First Avenue—Mile 18—with a large contingent of friends and family members. Daniel would desperately need her help to stand a chance of getting off the ropes.

Nancy flipped open her cell and listened carefully to Ken, pressing the phone against her ear so she could hear him above the boisterous crowd. He and Mike had called regularly with progress reports from along the course, and she'd been expecting another update, thinking Team Danny might be close. While waiting for them to arrive, her group—it included Danny's Uncle John and Aunt Paula, his cousins, and a bunch of friends from DMF and elsewhere—had been in a festive, jovial mood, cheering all the Marathon runners as they handed them pretzel rods and bananas. John had been booming out jokes as usual, and Nancy had joined in the laughter.

But now she was silent, her brow creased in thought. Ken told her Daniel was tiring, and he sounded concerned. The team would reach her in a few minutes—did she think she'd be able to get hold of what they needed?

She assured Ken she would and put away the phone, then turned from the course to start uptown through the mass of humanity on the sidewalk. She didn't want to waste a minute.

"Where are you going, Nancy?" one of the relatives asked.

"To get some chicken soup," she said. Nice, *hot* chicken soup. With plenty of salt.

A second later, she hastened off into the crowd.

———————

As Team Danny approached Ninetieth Street, they could see Nancy's group behind the barricade rails. They were jumping up and down, waving, and snapping pictures with their cameras.

Holding Danny by his arm, Ken broke into a grin. There out in front of the others was Nancy herself, holding a cardboard takeout container, a couple of large plastic bags at her feet. She'd gotten hold of their secret weapon . . . in abundance, from the looks of things.

The time Team Danny spent regrouping there on Ninetieth almost felt like a NASCAR pitstop. Nancy hurriedly poured salt into the chicken soup from little takeout packets, stirred it in with plastic spoons, and handed the containers and spoons to Daniel, his teammates, and the volunteers.

Ken couldn't remember chicken soup ever having smelled or tasted so good. The warm combination of rice, chicken, fat and salt revitalized Daniel almost instantly, bringing the color back into his face. He devoured it hungrily, hugged his mom, changed his shirt, hugged his mom, stretched, hugged his mom . . . and then gulped down more soup.

Fifteen minutes later Daniel's team assembled to get back on the course.

Ken took hold of his arm. "Think you're ready?"

A single nod.

"Definitely," Daniel said.

———————

Powered on chicken soup, hugs, and determination, Team Daniel entered the Bronx—the home of Daniel's beloved New York Yankees—and blew right past the infamous twenty-mile mark known as a brick wall to runners, the point where their reserves of energy tended to evaporate, and their bodies shut down. After a mile through the Bronx, they were over the Madison Avenue Bridge and back in Manhattan, turning down Fifth Avenue along the eastern border of Central Park.

Daniel's friends from Dalton had set up a cheering section on 107th Street, and they erupted into excited whoops and howls as the team passed. Spread out along Fifth, friends from DMF stood shouting encouragements and waving signs in the air.

Team Danny was now coming up on Central Park's Ninetieth Street entrance, the park to their right, its bare trees rustling in the November breeze, the staid old apartment buildings of Fifth Avenue on their left. It was the twenty-three-mile mark, and the fifth mile since their stop with Team Nancy. It was also where Ken had wheeled Daniel for their first Achilles walk, and where they had met their fellow walkers once or twice a week thereafter for the better part of a decade. Karen Lewis, the head of Achilles Kids, would meet them there for the last three miles to the finish line. The final push. It only seemed right that she be with Team Danny at that moment.

Thinking he didn't want to leave anything to chance, Ken reached for his cell phone to call Nancy again.

"I'll take another dozen cups of chicken soup, please," Nancy said. "With extra salt."

The counterman at the Triple Decker Diner looked across at her. She'd entered with her group moments earlier, and he had immediately come over to help them.

"Where're you meeting 'em?" he asked.

"Ninetieth Street and Fifth," she said.

He glanced up at the clock. "A dozen chicken soups, right away," he said, and hurriedly grabbed the ladle.

This time Daniel's team didn't stop for too long. A cup of soup each, hugs, high-fives, a warm exchange of greetings with Karen, and then off they went, back onto the course, back to the race, three miles left.

Three.

Ken's grip tightened on Danny's arm, and they exchanged silent looks. They were respectful of the race. They knew as well as anyone that things could happen in the blink of an eye. But they felt they were going to finish, truly felt it, their hearts and souls growing light beyond description with the feeling as they turned into the park and passed the Mile-24 marker, and then walked out onto Central Park South and across to Columbus Circle and turned back in. The finish line was in sight ahead of them now, the digital clock visible over a hill, ticking off each second from the start of the race. Their hearts light, so light, Ken glancing at Daniel, Daniel looking straight ahead, the rest of their team close around them, Ken's eyes suddenly blurring as he was overcome with emotion, tears dripping down Mike's cheeks, Kate Parkin crying now too, she'd seen Daniel move his big toe for the first time, his *toe* there on that hospital bed in Beth Israel, and now they were going to finish, *he* was going to finish . . .

Seven hours, forty-six minutes, and twelve seconds after he started, Daniel Trush walked across the finish line of the 2007 New York City Marathon.

Ken threw his arms around him.

Through flooded eyes, he saw an almost imperceptible smile on Daniel's face.

PART FIVE

HOPE AND BEYOND

CHAPTER TWENTY-ONE

The emailed invitations went out on July 13 and 14, 2011. Their subject line read, *Daniel's Music on Broadway.* This was what they said:

To our friends,

Hope all is well and that you are enjoying the summer! We have some very exciting news and have recently learned that a generous sponsor has donated the use of the Brooks Atkinson Theater (256 West Forty-Seventh Street where the musical "Rain" is currently playing) on Monday, July 25th from 1:00 p.m.–2:00 p.m. to DMF for our members to perform. Hard to believe that we have graduated all the way to Broadway! And if Broadway isn't exciting enough, we have also been informed that there will be some very special guests performing with our members (confidential)!

As always, the concert is free and we hope that you will be able to join us for this exciting event!

Seating for the concert is limited to friends of the DMF community, so please RSVP to us at danielsmusic.org or call us at—before Friday, July 22. Since this will be a private event, all attendees must be recorded on the guest list for admittance and should expect to arrive at the theatre no later than 12:30 p.m.

We hope that you will be able to join us on Monday, July 25! Warm regards,

Daniel, Ken, Nancy and Mike Trush

The Trushes and their unnamed sponsor had gone through weeks of preparation to make sure everything went off without a hitch that Monday.

They hadn't counted on the Broadway chaos, lost congas, and ice buckets. But as they knew all too well, you couldn't plan for everything.

The press conference room at Yankee Stadium in the Bronx, New York, was situated across the corridor from the team clubhouse in the stadium's massive and winding basement complex. The large raised podium at the front of the room was typically occupied by New York Yankees officials, coaches and players for question-and-answer sessions with the press; the lectern to its right was where Jason Zillo, the Yankees' head of public relations, most often stood presiding over the interviews. During press conferences, photographers for the news organizations would crouch before the podium with their cameras and flashes, while the wide area at the extreme rear was designated for television video crews. The long rows of chairs between the podium and television equipment were reserved for the journalists asking the questions.

Things were far from the norm at around 6:30 p.m. on July 25, as Daniel Trush and two DMF instructors, Brooke Bryant and Gerard Powers—Bryant had joined the staff in 2007, and Powers three years later—addressed the group of

DMF members and staffers occupying the room. In an hour or so they'd be performing DMF's syncopated, conga-driven rendition of the Star Spangled Banner for over forty-thousand Yankee fans there to watch the first in a series of games with the Seattle Mariners, assuming it ever stopped raining outside.

Bryant and Powers weren't overly concerned with the rain. They were musicians, not magicians, and the weather, inclement or otherwise, was out of their control. Their focus was on getting the performers ready, and part of that, a huge part, was making sure those performers weren't thrown off *their* game because the congas at the rhythmic heart of their stylized national anthem had gone AWOL.

How the congas went missing was that Ken, Daniel, Mike and Nancy, with the assistance of several members, had inadvertently dropped them off at Go Fish! en route to the ballpark, having been a mite too efficient bringing their instruments and equipment back from the Broadway theater where DMF and its "special guests" had performed for over a thousand invited supporters and national media representatives. And all that had happened thanks to a brainstorm by Artie Elefant, the early DMF member whose association with Daniel and Ken went back to their Achilles days.

Each year since 2009, the Yankees had planned a week of community outreach events to recognize individuals for having prevailed over obstacles that could have given them a plethora of reasons to fail, and who'd taken their experiences and used them as fuel for forward motion, impetus to help others in need. HOPE Week honorees—the acronym stood for Helping Others Persevere and Excel—were thrown a kind of daylong surprise party on a scale matching the sports franchise's iconic status and influence. The effort was Zillo's baby, an idea that had sprouted in his heart when he was still an intern with the Yankees, fusing his professional responsibilities with a desire to reach out a hand to do some good.

Daniel Trush's selection had been made months earlier. As DMF had grown, Elefant had been asked to join its pro bono advisory board as its outreach coordinator. A longtime Yankee fan—like Daniel—he'd thought HOPE Week offered a perfect way to spread awareness about DMF, phoned the Yankees' general switchboard, and asked for Zillo's office. Dolores Hernandez, Zillo's administrative assistant, had picked up and given him the steps for application.

Elefant had known there would be hundreds of viable entrants. But he felt that if he thoroughly presented the information about Daniel, his family, and their foundation, they would make a strong showing. By the spring of that year the foundation was offering twenty-six onsite classes and multiple offsite programs for individuals who could not easily travel to classes. Its members were doing outreach performances at schools, hospitals, nursing homes, and rehabilitation centers—Rusk among them. Its class list encompassed learning tracks for youths and adults, and for basic and more experienced students within the different age categories. There were five regular instructors as well as teaching assistants and members in leadership roles. The Musical Celebration concerts had outgrown St. Jean's in 2008 and moved to the four-hundred-seat Martin Theater at The Dalton School, which was donated for their use at only the cost of a security guard and maintenance worker.

Elefant had several exchanges of emails and phone calls with Hernandez as Daniel's candidacy was reviewed. Then a personal meeting with Zillo at Yankee Stadium in April, 2011, when Elefant happened to have tickets to a game. Zillo phoned Daniel and Ken the following day, and about two or three weeks later Ken was informed that Daniel would be one of that season's five HOPE Week honorees from among the many considered.

The Trushes and Elefant had been thrilled.

HOPE Week events combined a balanced mix of altruism and organizational pragmatism. The goals were to give the recipients a day to remember, advance their causes, and garner some good publicity for the Yankees. All Zillo typically knew from the start was that the events would be surprises, or a set of surprises, for the honorees and involve Yankee players who participated voluntarily. The creative thinking and nuts-and-bolts planning and strategizing were done in a series of blue-sky staff meetings in his office at the stadium. The grander and more ambitious the events, the better.

Zillo's research had told him the members of Daniel's Music Foundation learned music in their classes and performed at regular celebrations. What would be grander than performing on Broadway? Could the Yankees persuade a legitimate theater to offer its space?

Mondays were traditionally dark on the Broadway calendar because of Sunday matinees. The Brooks Atkinson on West 47th Street, one of the most prestigious theatrical houses in New York, offered to house the event on a Monday afternoon. The ball had gotten rolling.

On July 11, Ken and Nancy had met with Zillo at the Brooks Atkinson to make sure it offered wheelchair accessibility and full amenities for people with disabilities. Two days later, the Yankees and DMF had received clearance from the stagehands' union to open the theater on the off-day.

With only twelve days' left until the event, Ken had known it would be difficult to distribute physical tickets. After consulting with the theater's staff, he'd decided on an alphabetized guest list. The staff assured him complimentary tickets were distributed off a guest list every night and foresaw no problems.

Now DMF had prepared for the event.

Its instructors and students had a *lot* of show in them.

The playbill would read:

PERFORMANCE
AS FOLLOWS

Opening Remarks

Daniel's Thank You Song
Daniel & Gerry

All That Jazz
DMF Band

We Are Family
Adult Voice Technique Class

I Can
Youth and Adult Voice Classes

Larger Than Life
Super Six

You're The One That I Want
Youth Voice and Keyboard & Rhythm Class

New York, New York
Whole Company

The morning of the performance, Daniel, Michael, Ken and Nancy Trush had left their apartment at around 7:00 o'clock, jamming their car with instruments, equipment and cartons of playbills. At the Brooks Atkinson, a group of DMF staffers and people from New York Cares, a volunteer mobilization service that DMF had partnered with earlier that year, had descended on the car to unload it. They'd gone at the task like soldiers on a military operation and emptied everything out in five minutes.

The rest of the morning had been a cyclone of frenetic activity—the DMF staff setting up onstage, the performers getting into costume backstage. By nine or ten o'clock, the theater's front rows had begun to fill with media types jostling for interviews with the Trushes. Nancy famously eluded the spotlight. "My husband's over there near the stage with Daniel—they'll be happy to answer questions!" she told reporters. "Or my son Michael over *there* in the aisle! He can tell you everything about us!"

Even as the diverted press had swarmed Ken and Daniel, the Yankees PR team was introducing them to VIPs and guest performers who'd be joining DMF members onstage. Jennifer Steinbrenner Swindal, co-owner of the Yankees. The Latin pop star Romeo Santos. Broadway actors. Yankee players Nick Swisher, Russell Martin, Chris Dickerson, and Francisco Cervelli. The team's former centerfielder Bernie Williams, a lynchpin of four world championships, had launched a musical career as a guitarist after leaving baseball and volunteered to perform with the members. Williams had arrived to rehearse with Gerry Powers for *Daniel's Thank You Song* and his signature rendition of *Take Me Out to the Ballgame*.

Yankees radio broadcaster Suzyn Waldman would MC the performance. At 12:45, fifteen minutes before showtime, Ken had been backstage to discuss the program with Waldman and Zillo when someone called out that a mob scene was developing outside the theater. The theater's staff was having a problem locating names on the guest list. Their experience was holding tickets for people on one- or two-page guest lists. The Trushes' list was six or seven pages long and ticketless, and there was also a separate list of media arrivals prepared by the Yankees. Over a thousand names had to be checked off, and they'd been overwhelmed. People were backed up all along West Forty-Seventh Street.

Ken's automatic reaction had been to go outside and help—but then he'd realized that with only a few minutes until showtime, he'd miss the opening remarks introducing his family to the audience.

He'd tried to stay cool, reminding himself that when you were working with the disabled population, things popped up, and it was important to be patient.

"We shouldn't worry," he said. "It's a typical DMF event—organized chaos. Everything always works out."

Waldman had peeked out a side door.

"No," she said in a panic. "It's *pure* chaos out there! Chaos!"

Ken barely had time to consider that before he was told the curtain was about to rise. He would learn afterward that almost everyone got in on time . . . although *how* they did was something he'd never find out.

The introductions had rushed up on him before he'd known it. Then *Daniel's Thank You Song*, and the show-stopping *All That Jazz*, with Brooke Bryant onstage singing the lead, Danny soloing on piano with his right hand, and Nadine McNeil, who'd suffered two strokes in childhood and could only play with her left hand, at the keyboard beside him. Later in the proceedings, in emotional comments from the stage, Nadine—she was now DMF's program coordinator—would reflect that when she and Danny played together, they were whole.

The rest of the performance was an electrified blur for the Trushes. They would always remember their pride in the foundation's members, their joy at seeing them able to display their talents on Broadway, the inexpressible gratitude they felt for the opportunity, and the eager reception of the audience. At the close of the program, they were surprised by a giant check from the Yankees. And then Nick Swisher, the outfielder, told the crowd that DMF would be singing the national anthem at the stadium.

As the theater cleared out there had been more questions from reporters while the members and staffers packed away their instruments. More microphones, voice recorders and cameras. There had been correspondents from all the major television networks, as well as from print, radio and Internet news outlets—the New York Times, CNN, FOX News, ESPN and others . . . a very long list. Someone from Yankees PR had told Ken everyone would be heading back to the stadium, where the Trushes would have dinner before getting a tour of the ballpark. A section of field level seats had been reserved for DMF members so they could watch the game.

Ken had told the PR person he'd needed to return the instruments to Go Fish! and his apartment, and would head up to the Bronx once that was accomplished. Then he'd hastily joined everyone loading up the car. He had made it to the stadium without any problems.

As the rain had started to fall that afternoon, outdoor batting practice had been canceled. The Trushes had been shown the Yankee clubhouse and then led toward the indoor batting area to watch the players take their practice swings. Meanwhile, the instructors and members who would be performing the national anthem were escorted to the press conference room, which had been opened to them as a rehearsal space.

Ken was somewhere between the clubhouse and batting cage when one of the instructors appeared in the corridor, asking if anyone had seen the congas.

Congas? Ken had thought, whisked along toward the cage. Then it struck him that he hadn't brought them to the stadium. Amid all the excitement and commotion everybody had forgotten they were supposed to stay in the car.

"Hey! Danny, bro, *yeah baby*! Whaaassup?"

As Swisher came bounding over, Ken had stood there wondering how on earth the members were going to play their conga-driven national anthem without congas.

He'd turned to one of the television people, a producer from the team's broadcast network. "Do any of the players have congas?"

She'd given him a flummoxed look.

"Bongos?"

"I don't think so."

"*Drums?*" Ken asked, telling himself it wasn't so farfetched. The right fielder Paul O'Neill had supposedly kept a drum kit handy for when he needed to unwind.

The producer had looked at him another moment, shaking her head. O'Neill had retired a decade earlier. "Would ice buckets work? I could ask the clubhouse attendants."

Ken was thinking beggars couldn't be choosers. "Ice buckets sound great," he said.

She'd nodded and hurried to find out about the buckets. A few minutes later, they'd been handed to Bryant, Powers, and several of their fellow instructors, all of whom were in the press conference room with the performers, the entire bunch clad in Yankees paraphernalia and HOPE Week tee shirts.

"We don't play them any differently than the congas," Bryant told the group now, standing in front of the podium with her bucket. "It's the same as when we rehearsed."

"Think of them as homemade instruments . . . the congas *started out* being homemade instruments!" Braulio Thorne, a visually impaired percussionist interjected from his chair.

Bryant was nodding her head. "If you come in when you're supposed to, and start singing on your beat, you'll be fantastic."

"And remember to smile," Powers added from beside her. "If you're having fun, everyone in the audience will pick up on it, and they'll have fun. Piece of cake, guys."

Off to Bryant's right near the door, Daniel had listened quietly to their encouragements. Minutes before, he'd been up in the organist's booth playing *Take Me Out to the Ballgame* for the stadium crowd with his right hand. Then, as now, his smile was the definition of calm.

"Thank you so much, Brooke and Gerry," he said.

———

A few minutes before 9:00 p.m., after a rain delay lasting almost two hours, the Trushes and the DMF performers took the field for their rendition of the Star Spangled Banner.

With Martin, the team's primary catcher, preparing for the game, Daniel and Mike posed for some snapshots with Cervelli, Dickerson and the high-octane Swisher.

"Nice!" Swisher said after the flashes went off. He clasped both his hands around Daniel's. "Now we got it babe! Good job! We had an awesome time! *Awesome* time!"

Daniel and Mike both grinned.

Ken stood quietly watching them. During the brief pregame ceremonies, he'd watched a special message to his family from Gloria Estefan on the jumbotron screen, and then, along with Nancy and his sons, received the President's Volunteer Service Award at home plate. The Estefan video had given him a chill.

"Reach"

"I'm Not Giving You Up"

It had been fourteen years since he'd sat playing those songs to Danny from his hospital bedside. In some ways, it seemed so long ago. In others it might have been yesterday.

Ken inhaled, craned his neck back, and looked around at the great, sweeping curve of the stadium. It was crowded in spite of the delay, forty thousand fans, filling it to the upper deck.

And finally it was time. He stepped back as the members took their places for the anthem, Mike, Daniel and Nancy standing to his right, all of them lined up behind the performers.

Powers counted off. "One, two, three, and—" He clapped his hands to pick up the beat. A five accent, Bo Diddley-esque rhythm. One-two-three *four-five*, one-two-three *four-five* ...

The group sang, and the crowd joined in, all those voices blending with those along the first base line. *Oh say can you see by the dawn's early light.* One-two-three *four-five*. One-two-three *four-five*.

Jason Zillo, the public relations chief, had stayed on the field rather than take the elevator upstairs to the press box level. He'd wanted to feel the energy and he wasn't disappointed. Zillo had started out with the Yankees in 1996. He'd heard the anthem performed by dozens of highly acclaimed musical artists— people with beautiful voices, people who had a lot of polish. But he'd never felt an emotional reaction from the crowd as great as that night. He would always say it was one of the most memorable moments he'd had at Yankee Stadium.

The anthem neared its conclusion now. Powers signaled a rhythmic change and the drums stopped with a flourish. And then it was only the voices. The DMF performers, the crowd, the tens of thousands of voices, together:

Oh say, does that star spangled banner yet wave,
O'er the land of the free, and the home of the brave?

Swisher, the ballplayer, came pushing over to Daniel as the applause came pouring down from the stands, rolling over them in an avalanche.

"That's it, man," he said with an exuberant laugh. "That's *you* right there, bro. That's *you!*"

Ken stood quietly beside Nancy as Swisher threw his arms around Daniel's shoulders and embraced him, pulling him close to his brawny chest, hugging him so their cheeks were pressed together.

Then the public address announcer began calling the roll, and the PR team was guiding Daniel and Mike to the dugout, where they would pick up the Yankees' lineup card before Daniel showed it to the umpires and then threw the honorary first pitch.

Ken lingered outside only a few moments congratulating his members, then taking a final look at the stands from the perspective of the field, his gaze ranging upward from the lower deck to the top tier, and higher, rising above the stadium frieze to the night sky above.

In silent gratitude, he kept his eyes fixed there a moment, and then lowered them.

Time to move forward, there was much more work to be done.

DANIEL-ISMS

Daniel's Wit and Wisdom

Daniel often addresses large crowds at Daniel's Music Foundation (DMF) events. Before his first public speech, he tried to think of a way to summarize what happened to him and came up with this:

"I was in a coma for thirty days and in the hospital and rehab for a total of 341 days—*but who's counting?*"

His quip drew a big laugh. And like any incorrigible ham, he couldn't resist repeating it at speeches and presentations. Nowadays, in fact, it's become his signature. Audiences are so familiar with the line that they say it along with him each and every time he takes the podium....

But who's counting?

―――――――――――

As Daniel slowly emerged from his coma, Ken wrote his good-night song, and would repeat it to him every night as an expression of unconditional love and faith. Gradually, Daniel added his own words in response to his father's lyrics.

Ken continued singing the song to Daniel even after he'd returned home. For him it had become a warm, meaningful, and comforting interlude.

One night, Daniel looked up at him as he started in. "Can you please stop singing that to me?" he said.

Ken was taken aback. "Daniel . . . why now? After a year and a half?"

Daniel flashed his mischievous grin. "I couldn't tell you before—I was in a coma!" he said.

———————

After his discharge from Rusk, Daniel would return there daily for outpatient physical therapy. Each therapist also gave him a rehab routine to do at home. Determined to get him back to being the same person he'd been before his injury, Ken would push him very hard.

One day Daniel's face grew sad. Having rarely seen such a reaction from him, Ken asked what was wrong.

"I want you as my Dad, not my therapist," Danny replied "I have plenty of them and only one of you!"

It was a turning point for their relationship. At that moment, Ken realized Daniel wanted to be supported and accepted as he was and not as anyone else wanted him to be—and that included the people who loved him most dearly.

———————

Another time during Daniel's home therapy, Ken asked him his goal for that day.

"I don't set those types of goals," Danny replied. "I just try my hardest. Then I know I'll never be disappointed."

The words stopped Ken in his tracks.

Daniel had made an outpatient visit to Beth Israel a few months after his discharge and his neurologist inquired if he'd made any progress regaining his manual dexterity.

"So, Daniel, can you write?" he asked.

"Maybe if you gave me a pencil," Daniel replied, straight-faced.

Daniel's younger brother, Michael, had always looked up to him. But after Daniel's injury they underwent a role reversal. Mike took on so many responsibilities to assist with Danny's daily living activities, he in a sense became the big brother—although he still gave Daniel the kudos due him as the elder sibling.

Daniel would show him the same respect and appreciation. With characteristic humor, he labeled Mike his "bigger little brother."

Nowadays Michael introduces himself with that phrase when they meet people together:

"Hi, I'm Mike. Daniel's bigger little brother."

One day when Daniel and Ken were getting in shape for the Marathon, Ken told him, "Tomorrow you're going to have go fifteen miles, which will take you over four hours."

Knowing it marked a major intensification of their training regimen's time and distance, Ken waited for him to protest.

Daniel's answer surprised him. "That's what you've got to do, if you want to do the Marathon!" he said.

When the Trush family was setting up Daniel's Music Foundation, they sat down with their closest advisors to discuss the kinds of metrics they would use to gauge the program's success. A number of ideas came up at the meeting, but none of them seemed right or adequate. At last, Daniel suggested simply:

"I want to use a 'Smile-o-meter.' I want to judge it based on the number of smiles."

Naturally, everyone smiled.

The Smile-o-meter has been used every day at DMF since it opened its doors, and its readings are always sky high.

Although Daniel no longer has a formal physical therapy routine, he and his father continue to work out together. One day when Ken was showing him a new exercise to strengthen his stomach and leg muscles, he instructed him to stand up from a sitting position on a chair, arms extended straight in front of him. Then he stood facing Daniel.

"Keep your eyes on mine," he said. "That way we'll be sure to stay directly opposite each other."

Danny followed his instructions to the letter and locked eyes with his father.

"What's next?" he asked. "Are we going to tell each other our feelings?"

Ken was in a reflective mood one day, thinking about his boys getting older and more independent. Like so many parents, he'd been dedicated to their happiness and derived much of his personal fulfillment from watching them thrive. His thoughts led him to contemplate whether he'd change anything about his life if he got a mulligan—a chance for a do-over.

His family had been through wars together, facing many challenges. Things hadn't been easy for them. But their love and closeness was irreplaceable to him. He decided he'd take the hand he'd been dealt.

When he asked Nancy how she'd react to the same offer of a second chance, she told him she'd also keep everything as it was. They had a blessed life, with two great kids, she said. Why tinker with any aspect of it?

It was no coincidence that Ken had posed his question while Daniel was in the room. Although he'd been wondering how Danny would answer it, Ken hadn't wanted to skew his response by putting him on the spot. So instead he'd asked Nancy in his presence, leaving it for him to decide whether to comment.

Out the corner of his eye, Ken noticed that Daniel had listened to his mother's reply with perked interest. Clearly he was considering the question. Sure enough, when Nancy was finished, he chimed in, "I wouldn't change anything, either."

Ken looked at him with moderate surprise. "Not even the aneurysm?" he asked. "Wouldn't you rather have done without that?"

Danny was quiet for a long moment, his eyes serious. "If the aneurysm hadn't happened," he said slowly, "I probably would have become a businessman or lawyer. But there are plenty of those around, and Daniel's Music Foundation wouldn't be here today. When I think about all the lives it changes and all the joy it gives people . . . no, I wouldn't want anything to be different."

Nancy and Ken just looked at each other, floored by his declaration.

DMF's administrative office is currently in a separate room of the Trushes' apartment and has a dedicated phone. When Ken is in another room and hears it ring, he usually drops everything and hustles into the office to answer.

Ken was showering one day when Daniel walked into the bathroom with the DMF phone, held it out, and said, "Dad, this person would like to make a donation."

Dripping wet, Ken wrapped a towel around his waist, took the phone from him, and spoke to the potential donor—who had a lot of questions. Afterward, he was somewhat frustrated with Daniel for answering the phone and then giving it to him in the middle of his shower.

"Daniel, why did you pick up the phone?" he asked firmly. "Why didn't you just let it go to voicemail?"

Daniel turned to him, looking apologetic, "Dad, I'm sorry," he said. "But I'm just trying to be like you."

Tears welling up in his eyes, Ken was speechless. He could think of nothing to say.

Daniel's "thank-yous" are legendary. Since his injury, Danny has spread them around New York the way Johnny Appleseed once planted apple orchards across the frontier.

No nice word or gesture, no small act of kindness, caring or generosity, no small effort made on his behalf—or that he's seen a person do for someone else—goes by without a thank-you. Whether it's someone holding a door open for him, a server in a restaurant pouring him another glass of water, or a DMF volunteer going home at the end of the night, he likes to show his gratitude with those two small words.

When he ran the NYC Marathon, he must have said "thank you" over a hundred times to onlookers shouting encouragements along the route. The purity and sheer genuineness of his appreciation is always felt on the receiving end.

One day, Daniel had been coming down with a bug and felt fatigued and a little dizzy. As he laid down on the couch, Ken brought him a blanket and pillow. Naturally, Daniel gave him a trademark "thank-you."

"Daniel," Ken said, "you aren't feeling well. I'm your father. And I brought you a blanket. You don't have to thank me for it."

Daniel looked straight up at him, his head on his pillow. "It really doesn't take much to say those two small words, Dad," he said.

———————

Ken and Nancy have heard Daniel say hundreds of wise and funny things over the years. But the Daniel-ism they cherish most came in response to a question from the younger brother who'd always seen him as a hero.

The Trushes were together in their apartment shortly after Danny's hospitalization and rehab. Thinking of his yearlong ordeal, Mike had asked, "If you could be anyone else in the world, who would you choose?"

Daniel answered without hesitation. "I know who I am and I like it."

They were words his family never forgot.

AFTERWORD

The genesis of this book, and my proud friendship with the Trush family, goes back to July 25, 2011—the day Daniel became a New York Yankees' HOPE Week honoree.

At that time I was the unofficial point man for the YESNetwork.com's written HOPE Week coverage. The week's first recipient would be a young man named Daniel Trush. His story was irresistible. He wasn't supposed to live and he lived.

The Yankees' surprise to the Trushes also seemed nifty. Daniel and Daniel's Music Foundation members would be performing at the Brooks Atkinson Theater, a splendid Broadway playhouse. After introducing myself to the Trushes following the performance—Nancy, then Daniel, Michael and Ken, in order—I explained to Ken that I'd be tagging along with the DMF contingent as they toured Yankee Stadium.

I was hanging out in the press box later when I either noticed or was informed that the Trushes were being shown around the various control and broadcast booths on that same level. It seemed like a good time for our conversation.

As Ken had spoken of how his family had weathered their almost unimaginable crisis, I'd kept thinking there was something different and unique about the Trushes' way of handling it. A quality about Ken's and Nancy's approach to coping with and solving problems. It seemed to be rooted in faith and love—and not the lip-service variety. It was dawning on me that theirs was a quiet, nonjudgmental faith, a gentle and generous love.

Ken had blown me away ... and made me curious. What had inspired him to play music to Daniel from his bedside? To express his love for him by way of song lyrics? Had anything in his professional or personal background prepared him for the situation? I wanted to understand what made him tick.

Turning off my recorder, I said, "This next question isn't really for my story. But what makes you the way you are?"

Ken just looked at me. I'd known it was probably among the worst questions I could have posed. Besides being far too broad, it's unfair to ask someone to characterize himself in that way. Somehow, though, I'd been compelled to ask anyway.

After a few seconds, Ken shrugged. "I don't know," he said. "This is just us. We're just living our lives."

Us. *Plural.*

With the Trushes it's always about family. Their genealogical family, and their extended DMF family.

Before we ended our conversation, Ken asked if I'd be interested in doing something together in the future. None to my surprise, we began to tentatively discuss writing a book, and soon realized we all shared the same vision. We really just wanted to tell their story. It's still what we all want. That day at

Yankee Stadium was what Ken and his friend Chan Suh would call a game-changer.

As this book goes to press, DMF is moving from the rented studio space the Trushes have utilized from its inception to a new home on 101st Street and Lexington Avenue in Manhattan. It will occupy an entire floor of a tall modern building and offer state-of-art rehearsal studios, a recording studio, and a café for its members. It will go from having programs three days a week to six.

DMF is growing, changing, evolving.

But having spent many hours talking to the Trushes about it, though, I know their approach hasn't changed a bit. Their joy in the foundation's growth springs from being able to help greater numbers of people and better serve their membership. They are still about faith, love, and sharing their family's blessings with others.

Getting to know them has been a gift, writing this book with them an honor.

It is with profound appreciation and gratitude that I've shared their story with you.

—Jerome Preisler
July, 2013